W9-AUC-492

Spirit and Technique

IKEBANA

Spirit and Technique

Shusui Komoda
and
Horst Pointner

BLANDFORD PRESS
LONDON · NEW YORK · SYDNEY

First published in hardback in the UK 1980 by
Blandford Press, an imprint of Cassell Plc,
Artillery House, Artillery Row,
London SW1P 1RT

Reprinted 1983
Reprinted 1985

This paperback edition first published in the UK 1987
Reprinted 1988

First published in German as *Ikebanapraxis*
World Copyright © 1976 Verlag J. Neumann-Neudamm KG, Melsungen
Colour plates world copyright © Shufunotomo Co. Ltd

Distributed in the United States
by Sterling Publishing Co.,Inc.,
2 Park Avenue, New York, N.Y. 10016

Distributed in Australia
by Capricorn Link (Australia) Pty Ltd,
PO Box 665, Lane Cove. NSW 2066

British Library Cataloguing in Publication Data

Komoda, Shusui
  1. Flower arrangement, Japanese
  I. Title II. Pointner, Horst
  745.92′252   SB450
  ISBN 0 7137 1980 X

Printed in Portugal by Printer Portuguesa

ACKNOWLEDGEMENTS

Thanks are due to Ingeborg Beck, Monika Paul, Edith Seitz
and Anneliese Vitense for their valuable assistance, as well
as to the Shufunotomo Publishing Company, Tokyo, for
their co-operation and for having made available off-set
films for the colour plates 1–18, 20–30 and 32 as well as for
the loan of the photographs to lessons 22, 24, 29, 53, 58, 60
(4 each) and 23 (2).

All other photographs and drawings contained in this
book were made available by the authors. Ikebana
arrangements without the name of the artist were created by
Shusui Komoda. Translation from German by Eileen
Baum and help by Hilde Woodman-Gerlach in preparation of this edition are gratefully acknowledged.

PREFACE

Ikebana, the art of arranging flowers, which is practised in my homeland, Japan, has in the last few years continued to find enthusiasts in the West.

I am very happy to have been able to contribute something to this success, and I should like to thank all those who have encouraged me to teach and to go on lecture tours, as well as all those who have listened to my suggestions so open-mindedly, accepted them enthusiastically, developed them and passed them on.

My thanks go to the press for the hundreds of affirmative newspaper articles and to the television networks for having given me the opportunity through more than ten broadcasts to present Ikebana to a greater number of interested people.

The present volume can be of help to those wishing to learn Ikebana through a self-study course, and it can also be of use to advanced students wishing to deepen their knowledge. The aim of this book is also to show that Ikebana is more than just decorating shallow bowls with a few flowers, branches, or fruits. It should ultimately serve another important purpose. I should like to point out that, although Ikebana developed in Japan, it can be learned and understood by Westerners. Fifteen years of teaching experience in Europe have convinced me of this.

The most important Ikebana masters such as Ikenobô-Senei, the late Fujiwara Yûchiku, Kashô Kaneko, Murata Koushû from the Ikenobô School, Isseki Kusunoki, Kobayashi Shishû, Kumada Kôshu, Shimizu Kôho from the Saga School, Ikeda Masahiro, Ikeda Riei from the Koryu School, Ohara Hôun, Goshima Taiun, Oda Shûko, Yagi Toshi of the Ohara School, as well as Teshigahara Kasumi and Teshigahara Sôfû of the Sôgetsu School, have made photographs of their work available for this book. It is an honour for me to be able to thank them most kindly.

Shusui Komoda

A European, married to a Japanese as I am, continually experiences within the framework of his own family life the overlap of interests which exists between East and West, but he also becomes conscious of differences resulting from diverse backgrounds and philosophies of life.

For this reason, I began many years ago to contemplate writing an Ikebana textbook together with my wife. I felt it should encompass certain facets of Western art while, at the same time, emphasizing cultural values which have been developing in Japan for more than 1400 years.

After several years of planning and revision we present a well-balanced curriculum of Ikebana studies. For all those who cannot attend our personal lessons, demonstrations or seminars, we present numerous explanations, sketches, pictures and tables, starting with simple compositions, rules and hints and ending with rather complicated lessons.

Although we are very happy about the unexpectedly successful outcome of this textbook, we believe that the best approach to Ikebana is possible by direct experiences with nature, a quiet communication with plants and a sensitive understanding through your hands and heart.

Horst Pointner

Puchheim, Munich
Autumn 1979

CONTENTS

WAYS OF APPROACHING IKEBANA

Why shouldn't Westerners be able to learn and understand the Japanese art of flower arrangement as thoroughly as the Japanese understand Western art forms? It has been maintained again and again that a European can never really understand the essential nature of ikebana. We reject this contention. For the non-Japanese there are numerous ways of gaining access to this art form.

A purely intellectual approach, however, will not be completely successful. In the first section of this book, we think it necessary to say a few words in explanation of traditional Japanese aesthetics, the love of flowers there, the concept of Ikebana and the history of its several styles.

But you, dear reader, in picking up this book, have chosen a better approach, namely the way that leads through the senses. Didn't you first of all look at the photographs, enjoying the colours and forms of the plants, the movement of a line, or the contour of a leaf's edge? Take another look at the flower arrangements. Linger a while longer, but wait before beginning to read the text. Wait before asking yourself 'why?'. Read further only after you have brought a fresh branch into your room, feeling its leaves between your fingers, enjoying its fragrance after having placed it in a vase.

ENJOYING FLOWERS

It is not a special privilege of the Japanese to love flowers and plants. All over the world flowers are an essential part of festive celebrations, all over the world people give each other gifts of flowers, all over the world children pick flowers enthusiastically. A simple bouquet is to be found even in the remotest corners. In the ancient civilizations of Egypt and Crete, flowers were offered to the nobles.

1

Obviously this so-called 'pre-ikebana' is not an isolated phenomenon to be found only in Japan.

In the Middle Ages, monks, in addition to planting medicinal herbs and vegetables within the monastery walls, also grew flowers to decorate their altars. At this time wild roses, carnations, lilies, irises, garden peonies, violets, poppies, periwinkles, pansies and columbines were especially appreciated.

Scientific interest in flowers was given new impetus in the fifteenth century. Faraway lands and new parts of the earth were discovered, and from these many rare flowers and plants were brought back to Europe. At the courts of Europe, collections of paintings dealing with themes of natural history began to appear. In Padua, in 1543, the first European botanical garden was founded and many followed. Enthusiasm for flowers continued to grow as the Spaniards invaded Mexico in 1521 finding magnificent gardens in the palaces of Montezuma. Sunflowers, garden balsam, nasturium as well as the African marigold, were imported at this time. In the second half of the sixteenth century, envoys brought tulips to Europe from Turkey and they remained a fashionable flower of the first order for many years. Even up until the end of the seventeenth century a regular tulip-mania, consuming fortunes, prevailed in England, France and Holland.

High prices were paid at the beginning of this century for the Crown Imperial originating in Persia. At that time, the price of just one blossom equalled the cost of feeding a whole family for one year. This evil-smelling flower was first brought to Vienna from Constantinople by the botanist Charles de l'Escluse in 1576.

The story of a doctor, Noel Caperon of Orléans, illustrates the passionate interest of the times for botany. Caperon had discovered the fritillary near his home town. Being forced to flee to England after the St. Bartholomew Night Massacre (1572), he carried the flower with him in his suitcase, and, in this way, introduced it to the British Isles.

The first annual international flower exchanges, at which exotic flowers and seeds were speculated on, took place in the first half of the seventeenth century. A hundred years later hyacinth-fever broke out on the English market. In 1760, the King of England bought hyacinth bulbs for £100 apiece. Later, it is reported, he paid as much as £150 to £200 apiece.

Dealing in flowers, collecting valuable botanical rarities, creating gardens as well as presenting luxurious bouquets, were at this time the exclusive privileges of the nobility and the emerging bourgeoisie, while serfs fought for the right to fish and elect their representatives freely. But even among the peasants, colourful bouquets, dried flowers and budding branches were brought into the house on the occasion of religious feasts.

The Japanese art of flower arrangement saw a modification in several stages changing its style from a formal to a more natural one. At one time the will of the artist was most important, later it was the natural growth pattern of the plants. The same can be seen in European landscaping. In Goethe's time, the *Exotic Garden* in Weimar, which had been laid out in the strictly geometrical style of a French royal garden, was changed because it was felt to be old-fashioned. Leafy walks and circular paths, hedges and lanes had to make way for irregular meadows and bushes. Rare trees were planted and, even more important, the park was opened to the public. Up until this time, trees had served to adorn architecture and were subordinate to it. For Wilhelm IV, Duke of Weimar, who reigned from 1626 to 1662, the stately lime trees standing in the middle of his baroque garden didn't have enough of an artistic allure. For this reason, in 1650, he had a circular wooden structure set among them towering above the tree-tops. A spiral ramp led to the top of this peculiar structure and while ascending the ramp, one could observe through the windows the branches at the tops of the trees. The form of the trees could be seen and one could linger high above the tops enjoying man's ability to rise above nature. The prestige enjoyed by this interplay of nature and technology is shown by the fact that the 'snail' survived until 1808.

In Europe as well as in Japan, plants, especially flowers

and blossoms, were observed not only from a scientific, but also an aesthetic, point of view. Poetry and art lovingly adopted them. They were, and still are, used to give deeper meaning to events.

Among the first Westerners to learn to see Japanese plants through Japanese eyes were Engelbert Kämpfer, who was in Japan from 1690 to 1692, and Philip Franz von Siebold who worked there from 1823 to 1830 and then again from 1859 to 1862. For those of us who walk through botanical gardens today, the names of both of these scientiests greet us at every turn, Numerous plants which they brought back from Japan to Europe bear their names.

Enjoying plants in a simple and not at all scientific way can be one of the first steps towards ikebana. Is it possible that Westerners will develop an affinity for plants by handling them lovingly?

In East Asia the differences between living things are not felt so strongly as in Western culture. Plant life has never been considered as something quite different from human life. It is a part of the 'world harmony' to which man must once again return. Working with plants can help him attain this goal.

In order to carry on a dialogue with plants, it is not necessary to remember all that has been said up until now. It is so simple, just pick up a flower in your hand. If it is soft you will handle it tenderly, if it has thorns you will be careful! You enjoy the fresh colour, the satiny surface of the petals and its fragrance. Your eyes follow the curving lines of the blades of grass. A game played with the senses. Who can maintain that Westerners have lost the capacity for all that?

WESTERN ART

Western attitudes became superficially similar to those of Japan, independently of artistic developments in that country. An understanding of foreign ideas comes with the study of another culture's art forms, even if it is the novelty that is the first attraction.

Anyone who has been interested in ikebana for many years and who has met many people all over the world who have made ikebana an integral part of their lives, will certainly understand Leonardo da Vinci when he said that a base person would not be able to express anything more than his own baseness had he not sufficiently studied beautiful forms. The Japanese know this as well. They know that an encounter with the beauties of nature can affect the observer and influence his inner life.

Symbols are dependent upon one's views and frame of reference, but the ability to symbolize is cultivated in all cultures. Not only artifacts, but also nature's works have always been the objects of man's interpretation. The tree has been a symbol of life since time immemorial. It also represents the law. Blossoming plants always alluded to the presence of saints in the religious paintings of the Middle Ages. Such pictorial symbols were, at that time, of much greater significance than today, as the lower classes were still illiterate. In this way certain plants became symbols of status.

On the right-hand panel of the famous Catharine Altar by Lucas Cranach the Elder, in the Gemäldegalerie in Dresden, an angel is seen bringing roses to Saint Dorothy.

An angel in the form of a child, painted in 1506 for the church at Torgau, holds a small basket filled with red and white roses. The white roses symbolize purity while the blood-red ones symbolize Christ's Passion. In Japan as well, numerous flower baskets, often filled with chrysanthemums, are to be found in antique drawings, which are regarded as a form of ikebana. For lovers of European bouquets, the appearance of a similar art form in East Asia might be an interesting topic for investigation.

Albrecht Dürer took great pains when painting flowers. One would think he held his breath before the wonders of nature so as to perceive them only with his eyes. On a piece of paper in the Vienna Albertina, he drew a columbine beside a bunch of panicle grass. We find this delightful water-colour, painted in 1526, captivating because of its natural freshness. When we look at the gracefully formed bluebell flower buds, we have the feeling of entering deeper into the secrets of nature. The drawing speaks to us of modesty and solitude. We really feel that the plant at that time only grew far away from inhabited areas, in shady, humid meadows and on the edge of the forest. It was not without good reason that the buttercup at that time symbolized unrequited love. In the famous painting by Hieronymus Bosch, 'The World as a Haywagon', dry grass symbolizes the transitoriness of life. The lily is the pictorial symbol of innocence and purity.

Towards the end of the sixteenth century, the Dutch introduced the botanically correct, natural way of painting flowers. Using the magnifier they created the most beautiful collection of botanical paintings. Following the so-called 'Botanists' came the colourful series of 'Florists'. Using Jan Davidsz de Heem as their model, generations of Dutch artists painted bouquets of flowers and exported them around the world. A bouquet painted by de Heem gives one the impression of being a wild scrub. By using the principle of contrasts a baroque rhythm is obtained but no individual flower communicates anything to us. We would like to extricate at least one from the confusion of colours, so as to observe it more closely. This could lead to the Japanese way of looking at flowers.

Even in the Far East at one time, luxurious bouquets of flowers served to enhance the prestige of the ruling classes. As in Europe under the reign of Louis XIV, monumental floral still-lives decorated the chambers of the new palaces. Moreover, the flowers were twisted around each other, pressed and cut into pieces so that the image created was one of a rough pile of flowers. In both East and West, the desire for simplicity and clarity grew out of a predilection for pomp and splendour.

For Westerners, the ideas of Paul Cézanne may shed some light on the attitude of the Japanese towards nature. In his still-lives he attempted to bring out the 'purely artistic truth in things'. In this way, he reduced natural forms to simple cylinders, cones and spheres. In Japanese art as well, simplification is a main principle, but whereas Cézanne viewed art as a 'harmony running parallel to nature', the Japanese consider created beauty and natural beauty to be substantially the same.

Georges Braque seems to share the opinion of many Ikebana masters, even very modern ones, when he said, 'I work with material and not with ideas!' Doing comes first, only then can ideas follow. Action always serves as the basis for ideas, for conceptions. Today it is still the same: millions of Japanese have mastered the art of ikebana, but very few put their knowledge into words.

The influence of the Far East is already present in Van Gogh's work, which marks a turning point in nineteenth-century European art. Due to Commodore Perry's expedition in 1853 which brought about the opening up of several Japanese ports previously closed to foreigners, trade agreements were made and Japanese ceramics and woodcuts began appearing in the West. These products were found pleasing because of their exotic allure, which in turn gave rise to an anecdotal use of Japanese motifs in painting. All things Japanese became fashionable in France.

Edouard Manet's portrait of Emile Zola, in which a Japanese woodcut and a folding-screen appear, is an important document of an epoch during which Japanese motifs were incorporated into Europe's cultural horizon. Japanese art remained 'exotic' until the decisive works of

Van Gogh. Foreign motifs were inserted into a composition belonging completely to the European tradition. Van Gogh did not use the Japanese work of art merely as an additional motif, but rather as the composition's point of departure. In this way — at first for himself — he smoothed the way to understanding the principles and characteristics of Japanese fine arts. For Van Gogh, the Japanese woodcut served as a model for his love of those things, for his absorption in nature which make his later works so convincing. 'Is it not possible that we can see a thing that we love better and more correctly than something that we do not love?' he wrote to his brother. This is why Van Gogh experienced and portrayed roots more intensely than most of his contemporaries. And it is for this reason that he expressed more than just reality in these works. Roots led him to an interpretation of life. For those who have experienced this in European art, the access — however narrow — to the art of Ikebana is open.

It is seldom realized that collage is related to ikebana. This is certainly true concerning the way in which both are made. As in Ikebana, already existing materials are combined to create a new unity. The artist is constantly bound by the laws of the material itself, or at least he must take them into consideration. Whereas dead material may be handled heartlessly, flowers demand careful attention otherwise they will fade too quickly.

For the open-minded Westerner, the 'ready-mades' by Marcel Duchamp — just consider the common bottle rack of 1914 — offer access to yet another aspect of the Japanese art of flower arrangement. We learn here how an article of common use gains a new perspective by being exhibited in a museum. A change in perspective leads to a poeticising of the object. Characteristics become evident which had gone unnoticed before. The same is true of the single flower, found on the edge of a path, which now livens up the room.

Although the trend in art in Japan is unfortunately towards the development of an international style, sufficient cultural characteristics remain intact to inhibit a complete homogenization. Hidden behind external appearances (i.e.

traffic and clothing) enough traditional attitudes still prevail so that changes only take place slowly. These Japanese attitudes are becoming ever more obvious due to the active exchange of ideas and goods with the West.

One need not agree completely with Heinz Junker when he maintains that 'Europe comes from Asia', but it remains a fact that Japanese architecture has influenced the European. Gropius and Le Corbusier brought the sliding door and the idea of functional design from Japan. At the same time, push-open doors were being built into Japanese houses made of red brick in the European style. Westerners who want to understand ikebana should be aware of this exchange of ideas.

During the last 30 years artistic exchange has increased, Japanese art is shown abroad quite often. The Japanese are also very interested in exhibitions of foreign works, and this fact is readily seen by the large numbers of visitors attending such exhibitions. The *Japanese International Art Exhibition* which became famous under the name *Tokyo Biennale* is today the fourth largest in the world.

In Japan, as in Europe, it has been shown that one can recognize, understand and even love the artistic content and methods of another culture while continuing to accept the cultural tradition in which one lives. He who has no cultural home will not find one in the exoticism of ikebana. Ikebana is neither a refuge nor a pseudo-religion. It can, however, open up new areas of consciousness for Westerners at home in their own cultural tradition. It can mean an enrichment of their cultural outlook just as Western culture has meant an enrichment for Japan.

INTEREST IN JAPAN

Miracles arouse curiosity, and this is why some ikebana lovers from the West had read about Japan long before having attempted their first flower arrangement.

What kind of a country is it in which a manager after having concluded a contract for a 400,000 tonne tanker seeks the peace and quiet of a tea-house so as to enjoy its simplicity. What kind of country is it in which only eight lawyers serve 100,000 inhabitants. What kind of country is it in which, as long ago as one hundred years, a book with the title *An Admonition to Learn* sold 3.4 million copies?

Nowhere else in the world are such turbulent cities and such secluded, deserted valleys to be found so close to each other. Some say that the special affinity to nature of the Japanese stems from the continual danger of earthquakes. Sensitive instruments record approximately four medium disturbances daily. On an average of once a month, the earthquakes are so strong as to cause houses to shake. The strongest earthquake in modern times occurred on 1 September, 1923. It completely destroyed Yokohama and much of Tokyo. The annual typhoon, a tropical storm occurring between summer and autumn, continues to cause great material damage and human suffering. Less well known is the 'plum-rain' which falls evenly in June and July transforming the land into a green paradise. This *bai-u* in conjunction with the dry August weather is also responsible for the good rice harvest in Japan. A further geographical factor contributing to their closeness to nature, may very well be the fact that Japan is composed of 3325 large and small islands, the southern-most being covered with tropical vegetation.

Many Japanese doubt whether the cultural innovations ascribed to them in the *Encyclopedia Americana* are really the most important ones. These include the deep, hot bath, the whole complex of societal behaviour patterns, a characteristic unrhymed poetic form, and light delicate paper. The Japanese educational system is specially described in the *Bolschaja Sovjetskaja Enziklopedia*. People all over the world are interested in knowing how the Japanese manage to learn the 1850 symbols necessary for reading ordinary printed matter. In six years of elementary school alone, 881 different Chinese ideograms *(kanji)* have to be learned. Most of these symbols are made up of 10 to 18 components. The symbols for 'example' *(kan)* and for 'following' *(shu)* comprise 23 individual strokes. Astonishment increases when Westerners learn that, in addition to this, two-syllabic alphabets each containing 46 letters are also necessary. Before the war, it was even worse: 3000 to 5000 *kanji* were used in literary works. That learning to use this script represents a very effective way of training one's apprehension of forms as well as one's memory is a fact that no one will deny.

The studiousness of the Japanese is also evident in the field of music. In 1860 the first German musicians were heard in Japan. Forty sailors played *Ich bin ein Preusse, kennt ihr meine Farben?* (I am a Prussian, do you know my colours?). The road leading to an appreciation of European classical music was not an easy one, for the foreign music sounded like a confusion of noises to Japanese ears. It is said that in 1860 not one Western European instrument was to be had in Japan. Today, Tokyo is one of the leading music capitals of the world. The Japanese music audience is one of the most devoted in the world. Japan's piano manufacturers have been at the top of the world's list for a long time.

We still read here and there that Westerners can never understand Japanese art, let alone be able to reproduce it, but the facts just mentioned allow us to doubt these assertions. Fifteen years of teaching experience in the West has shown that Europeans are certainly able to master the art of ikebana as well as to understand all of the points of its intellectual content. For intuition is a talent belonging not only to Orientals, although it has been more carefully nurtured in the Orient throughout history than in the West.

Today, every Japanese is brought up in such a way that he will feel equally at home both in modern industrial society and in his traditional environmental structure. Here, two souls are not contained within one breast, as the Westerner often supposes, but rather both form a whole. The tension between the two cultures brings about a positive reaction, this being a further impulse towards progress. In this soil, a broad and strongly differentiated cultural life has been able to grow, which is in turn represented in the variety of modern Ikebana styles.

Who is surprised to learn that the largest wooden structure in the world, the Hall of the Great Buddha in Tôdaiji, near Nara, is in Japan? What a predeliction for the superlative! What a diversity of cultural forms! The world's fastest train, the largest tanker, the least delay among express trains — only 18 seconds delay per train — the largest chrysanthemum and the smallest blossoming and fruit-bearing cherry tree *(bonsai)* measuring only 4.8 cm.

Of course we hope that the fascination that Japan exercises on the Western mind, that the European's astonishment at the numerous achievements of this country, will not lead to exaggerated enthusiasm. An uncritical attitude towards the exotic on the part of Europeans is as painful to the Japanese as 'Madame-Butterfly sentimentality' or 'Geisha romanticism'. Only those who are able to maintain a certain objectivity, to recognize Japan's social and economic difficulties and the mistakes made in the country, will become a true friend of Japan and its culture. Such individuals will also be able to perceive those facets of Japanese culture which Europe has not cultivated with the same intensity; the art of flower arrangement is certainly one of these.

JAPANESE AESTHETICS

The term 'Japanism' signifies the influence of Japanese art on European art with all its ramifications. Enthusiasm for all things Japanese in the nineteenth century led to the collecting of Japanese arts and crafts. This was helped by the Meiji Reform, an event that obliged impoverished members of the nobility to sell their works of art. In 1883, Claude Monet designed his garden at Giverny along the lines of a Japanese model. It included a bridge, water plants and irises. From 1886 to 1888, Vincent van Gogh, as has already been mentioned, came to grips with Japanese woodcuts. His copy of 'Ôhashi-Bridge in the Rain' by Andô Hiroshige demonstrated the influence of Japanese aesthetics. Aesthetics deals with the appearance and value of beauty, but it is not a static discipline. Beauty is in the eye of the beholder. Aesthetic experience must be dynamic, i.e. capable of change, otherwise creative development in art would be blocked. Aesthetics do not come before art exists, but rather art itself always precedes the theory of beauty.

In Japan as well, aesthetics are constantly subject to change. The pure, unadulterated Japan exists only in the fantasy of Western writers, or in the works of Japanese scholars who want to protect their culture from what they believe to be harmful foreign influences. It is precisely this coexistence, this combination and interlocking of cultural traditions of different origins, which represents for us the original Japanese culture. Many visitors to Japan complain about the disappearance of romantic Japan in which Geishas in colourful kimonos, snow-covered Mount Fuji and cherry blossoms are the most important elements. They should, however, be happy that in Japan as well aesthetic values are subject to changes of interpretation. This development, as we are going to show in the course of this book, is evident in Ikebana. It is in this context that all the rules of the Japanese art of flower arrangement are to be understood. The Japanese themselves are open to new impulses from abroad as far as the composition of new flower arrangements is concerned. This is hardly possible if all that can be expected from abroad is a superficial and rigid obedience to the rules. Rules must remain living guidelines. Only when their meaning and effect on Ikebana arrangements has been understood, and we mean not merely understood with the intelligence, but with the hands, only then has a sound basis for the further development of Ikebana been created. The understanding that the intricacies of this art form cannot be mastered overnight in a speed course, but only after years of cheerful practice, and that mastery is only possible after years of effort, is one of the main objectives of our book.

When reading our presentation of some of the aesthetic aspects of Ikebana, the various interpretations of these concepts should be kept in mind. In the end, evaluation is left to the discretion of the observer. He is the one who perceives the positive values in these categories. It is for this reason that we have permitted ourselves to choose aesthetic categories which we feel are most important for Western art and to which we ourselves are most attached.

Harmony and elegance, simplicity and asymmetry, transitoriness and closeness to nature are areas of aesthetics which overlap at many points, which complement each other but never exclude each other. They are associated with ikebana but can also be extended to other art forms.

Today especially, there is no longer one ideal of beauty. In Japan too, a general consensus concerning aesthetic values disappeared in the nineteenth century. Don't we have any guidelines regarding what is beautiful today?

From the standpoint of Ikebana, there are still two, and one of them is nature. The field of aesthetics extends beyond that of the fine arts. Even in nature and in everyday life, for example in the field of sports, or in the non-cultural part of life, aesthetics plays a role. Since in ikebana we are dealing with nature, i.e. with living materials, it is only natural that the aesthetics of plants be included in our artistic creation. The further we move away from nature, the more uncertain becomes our evaluation of natural beauty.

For this reason, a further criterion is offered, namely, the consensus within the individual ikebana schools. Inasmuch as the *Ikenobô-Ikebana-School* is a historical entity, its guidelines are also subject to change. Exceptional masters have provided new or altered contents. Today the leading teachers meet at irregular intervals to analyse modifications which have taken place in the course of time. Sometimes new rules emerge organically from these meetings as if they had formed themselves. In 1958, for example, the rules governing Rikka were renewed and adapted to the needs of modern times. Four years earlier, the same institute (*Ikenobô-Bunka-Kenyû-Sho*) changed the rules for Shôka. Out of this emerged the Sanshuike-Shôka. Recently, Headmaster Ikenobô Senei developed the new form of modern Ikebana, the Shinputai, and published his ideas in 1977.

In Japan, the authority of the academies to set guidelines is generally not felt to be tutelage. Today, students can choose between almost 3000 different schools. The Ikenobô School alone numbers more than 1.5 million students a year, thus making it Japan's most popular ikebana school, despite, or because of, its rigour and adherence to tradition concerning curricula and examinations. Two of the larger, newer schools, Sôgetsu and Ohara, register approximately one million students.

Even in the twentieth century, individual standards of orientation are offered and accepted. Nature and master have remained the teachers.

8

Harmony

The master's extended observation of nature enables him to perceive the harmony which is its basis. Harmony is a characteristic of all Japanese art. This harmony is reflected in the work of the garden architect Sôami. This famous work of art has not been changed since the fifteenth century. Moss-covered rocks emerge like islands from a bed of fine gravel. A weathered mud-wall encloses the area. Visitors sit silently but serenely on the wooden veranda of the Ryôanji Zen-Temple in Kyôto. The colours of the wood are repeated in those of the wall, the deep green of the moss-patches in the foreground has the same effect as the tree-tops in the background. Rocks, gravel and stepping stones seem to belong to the same family. Although aesthetic pleasure is not the main aim of a Zen garden, the aesthetic moment is reached when one questions nature about the position of man in the cosmos. The observer feels himself drawn in by the harmony of colours and feels himself to be at one with the universe.

Balance of accentuation and significance in the thickness and curvature of the lines are qualities that make calligraphy, the art of fine handwriting, valuable. Each Chinese ideogram is a microcosm in itself. *Wa* (harmony) is the principle on which penmanship is based. The movement while writing and the symbol which is formed on the paper both affect the writer. In this way, harmony while writing can lead to harmony of personality, in the same way that people with unbalanced characters have inharmonious handwriting.

Since Shôtoku-taishi (572–621), the spirit of *daiwa* (great harmony) is also an integral part of Ikebana. This is developed through the gentle handling of flowers. The artist recognizes the growth pattern of the plants and has to bring his desire to create into accord with the plants' peculiarities. Unity of beauty in art and nature emerges in Ikebana and thus harmony in turn affects the artist. Within him a 'gentle resonance' *(yojô)* springs up. This 'positive sensation' can perhaps be conveyed even in the translation of a poem by the noble Zen follower Fujiwara Sada'ie (1161–1241):

> *The scent of the plum*
> *On my sleeve*
> *Competes with the moon rays*
> *Dropping through the roof.*

Especially in classical ikebana, *yûgen*, the inexpressable quality of a harmonious work of art, is revealed. Here something unfathomably deep, something exceptional and of particular beauty reveals itself. When speaking about such concepts, or when trying to explain them as we have been doing here, it all sounds rather pathetic. One should forget about speaking, direct experience is the most important thing.

Harmony is most easily attained through repetition. The serenity and openness of a chrysanthemum blossom is reflected in the eye of the artist, as soon as he surrenders himself without reservation to the flower. The curved line of the mountains on the horizon outside the window of a Japanese home is in unison with the movement of the pine branch of an ikebana composition inside the house. Autumn outside, autumn in ikebana, and maturity of the artist, this would be a completely harmonious triad. Form and colour, flowers and branches, blossoms and leaves unite harmoniously with the container and the room, with the season and with the sentiments of the artist. Only in modern Ikebana may we forget the principle of *wa*. Here dissonance appears. The harmony of nature is, however, underscored through this principle.

Certainly it remains Utopian to believe that through the principle of *wa* in ikebana, the principle of *hei-wa* (peace, literally 'peaceful harmony') will emerge in the world. In 1970, on the occasion of the Osaka World Exhibition, 77 nations using the plum blossom as their symbol attempted to show their conceptions of the 'way to progress and harmony for mankind' and how they could attain this.

Fûryu

He who is able to gain access to *fûryu,* an Oriental-Buddhistic harmony of the spirit, need no longer talk about the meaning and purpose of an act. He need not indulge in philosophical speculation. His ikebana is fûryu. Fûryu is something tasteful, worthy but not opulent. Fûryu is the elegance of imperfection. Ikebana is understood as *fûryu no asobi,* 'elegant enjoyment'. A branch which cannot grow directly towards the light, which is curved and bent, which only bears a few buds instead of a mass of blossoms, this branch is then fûryu. That no exact translation of this expression is possible indicates a difference between Eastern and Western attitudes.

Simplicity

The most powerful works of traditional architecture radiate simplicity. Even from masters who construct large flower arrangements, simplicity is demanded. *Wabi* and *sabi* are the distinguishing characteristics of Japanese works of art. Again, we are not in a position to give adequate translation to these concepts. They may be closest to the ideas of solitude and fragility. Do you remember the meaning of ikebana? Plants should be shown to their best advantage. But buckets full of roses and carnations do not bring out the flowers' grace. Getting down to essentials should be practised by means of simplification and restriction. A single flower properly presented can bring an entire summer day into the home. Less is more. Suzuki once said: 'One blade of grass is enough to determine the direction of the wind.' Who has not already come to the realization that a long speech hardly says more than only the hint of a gesture. It is often only a question of one point of view. A short, charming Japanese poem illustrates this.

> *When I lie in the grass*
> *Near Musashi*
> *The tiny flower*
> *Seems larger than Fuji.*

An important element of ikebana is the principle of uncluttered space. Only with such a background can the power of a line be felt. It is that which has been left unsaid that excites the mind of the observer. The empty spaces of a pen and ink drawing are positive and indispensable means of expression. The observer's fantasy is inspired by the sense of freedom conveyed by the mist and clouds left unrepresented. Sesshû (1420–1506), a talented Zen painter who was sent to China to study, laid down the guidelines for all later pen and ink drawings. Two of his exceptional landscape panoramas still exist. On scrolls more than 16 metres long, he created panoramas of water, mountains and snow-covered temples. Such reserve, such subtle simplicity! Only a few brush strokes are needed to create a tree bent by the wind, and the fissured cliffs underneath. Ships move towards the cliffs in a fog. Far off, mountains barely hinted at emerge through the delicately painted sky.

Chinese art and architecture of the T'ang-Dynasty were once the most important models for Japan. This is especially evident in the eighth century when the capital, Nara, was laid out according to Chinese plans. The characteristic curved roofs were covered with green bricks. Columns were painted red. The grand gestures and love of display were repeated inside the houses as well. But even as early as the beginning of the Heian Period (794–1192), when the capital was transferred to Kyôto, tastes began to change. The simplicity and smoothness of earlier art was once again acknowledged. Roofs were once again covered with shingles of bark instead of glazed bricks. In the interior of buildings restraint was once again practised, the luxury of rich colours renounced. Preference was again given to simple, untreated natural wood, its natural colour setting it off most advantageously. From the tenth to the twelfth centuries, the distinctive characteristics of Japanese expression developed.

Delicacy, dignity and elegance became the prevailing qualities in all artistic expression. The derivative style in Europe was replaced in the twentieth century. In 1919, in Weimar, the Academy of Fine Arts and the School of

Applied Arts combined to form an arts institute which soon determined the direction of artistic endeavours, namely the Bauhaus School.

The architecture department directed by Walter Gropius attempted to integrate the new artistic concepts coming from Japan. Thanks to the influence of the Bauhaus School, above all in the area of art education where it is still felt today in European design, values such as clarity, objectivity, practicality and simplicity once again became fashionable. A special feature of this school is its responsibility for including objects of common use and forms of technology under the title of artistic creations. Famous artists were produced by the Bauhaus School — Feiniger, Itten, Marcks, Muche, Schlemmer, Moholoy-Nagy, Klee and Kandinsky.

For this reason we believe that simplicity as an aesthetic principle of Japanese art is easily acceptable to Westerners seeking access to the Japanese art of flower arrangement.

Asymmetry

For the Japanese, symmetry is felt to be all too static. Symmetry affects people like a law that has been forced upon nature. Just think of the overfilled bouquets of the Baroque era. There is no room for one's own thoughts. The eye runs bewildered from flower to flower. It is precisely the form which is not enclosed on all sides, the form with open spaces, that excites the eye to explore. The incomplete asks to be completed. All things which appear incomplete and unfinished symbolize life's dynamics.

A prominent feature of Japanese painting and of the art of flower arrangement is its lack of frames. The perspective in Japanese genre paintings appears infinite and disappears without transition into the painting's background. In this way, space and landscape are blurred in the emptiness of the picture's surface increasing the expressive power of the motif. We rarely find any kind of symmetry in these works.

The varied dimensions of depicted space convey a feeling of dynamism.

In architecture and landscaping, symmetry was deliberately avoided. The periods were comparatively short during which buildings were constructed in the Chinese *kara-yô* style. Within a short time, the symmetry of temple landscaping no longer corresponded to Japanese tastes. Individual homes and sacred buildings were once again asymmetrically laid out. Passageways of various heights and breadths connected the buildings. A focal point was not aimed at in such a layout, and a central axis was absent. Even the royal villa Katsura near Kyôto, built in the seventeenth century, was constructed according to this principle. The observer notices the elegance with which every kind of symmetry has been avoided. A feeling of lightness and openness is obtained here through a rhythmical combination of the elements.

In Japanese homes of all classes , symmetry is hard to find. The walls are divided up into uneven panels, and asymmetry gives individuality to each section. The upright timbers of the *tokonoma,* the alcove frame is left rough, the grain and the knots do much to enliven the interior. The result is asymmetry. No two windows are built at the same height, nor are they the same size, at least not in the same room. This is why the Western visitor perceives the Japanese home, in spite of its calmness, as a living organism and not as a rigid cage.

In Ikebana we always strive towards creating an unequal triangle. It is infinitely variable and expresses something of the dynamism and variety of life. Nothing is definitive, everything is in flux. *In* and *yô* are never really brought into a state of equilibrium. Sometimes one predominates, and

Asymmetry in Rikka

Symmetry in a bouquet

then the other. Man *(jin)* tries to obtain a balance between the forces of sky *(ten)* and earth *(chi)*. This is the actual source of human creativity.

Closeness to Nature

Flowers are a symbol of nature's creative powers and there is no doubt that people who practise the art of ikebana have a special relationship to nature. In other Japanese art forms as well, closeness to nature is more apparent than in Western arts. In the Orient, nature and culture are not felt to be opposites. For the Japanese, culture has always been regarded as a gift of nature. Seen from this point of view, Western art seems to feel itself compelled to surmount natural models. The term 'remoteness from nature' has been used to describe the European Middle Ages. Neither the size nor the spatial relationships in the artistic works of that time reflect the actual human environment. Certainly, men, animals and plants are portrayed but in a subjective relationship to each other. They ask to be *read*. The feeling 'of being part of nature' is never evoked by pictorial works of art of that time, by stained-glass windows of churches, by architecture, by panels nor by frescoes.

The Japanese home and even shrines and temples are so natural compared with Gothic architecture. Here, man is the yardstick for his environment. Natural forms, mountains, trees, ponds and lakes are repeated in the home. The home is part of nature. Through the openness made possible by Japan's climate, the occupant is able to take part in the change of seasons. In Japanese fine arts as well, the seasons are reflected. Scrolls *(kakemono)* hung in the niche of honour *(tokonoma)* are also changed so as to reflect the time of year. Ikebana too is always in harmony with the change of seasons. In Western art and especially in the flower still-life paintings of the Netherlands, one can often observe that painters like Jan Brueghel (1558–1625) try to unite all seasons in one painting. In his painting 'The Sense of Smell' we see irises, crowns imperial, snowdrops, water lilies, primroses, tulips and daffodils in one composition.

Snowdrops bloom in February, irises only at the begnning of June. Decoration — despite the master's genius — triumphs. The most important element is the plan, the artist's *idea*. Nature supplies the background and the raw material. Natural beauty is subject to other laws than artistic beauty.

Japanese history, on the other hand, has been influenced by a religion which places nature at the centre, namely *Shintoism*. It is said that Shintoism counts more than eight million deities. To these *kami* belong rivers, mountains, certain natural phenomena such as fire and water, and also warriors, thinkers and members of the imperial household. The feelings and beliefs of the Japanese are still influenced by this undogmatic religion. An ancient tree, held in position by many supports, stands in a temple precinct in Kyôto. Visitors see in this tree the miracle of life. In it they encounter the absolute. Traffic noises are blocked out for a few moments and the visitor once again becomes a part of nature. At such moments, reason and knowledge no longer count. All things required through learning, even morality, lose their meaning. *Kimochi,* a strong emotion, emerges — a feeling for nature. Mountains, an old fir tree and flowers speak a language that everyone understands. For Japanese sensibilities such thoughts are felt to be self-evident.

The fact that the Japanese have always valued highly the natural world may stem from the lack of available living space, from the ever-present mountains, from the feeling of being subjugated to the forces of nature by earthquakes and typhoons, and from the interaction of land and sea. Veneration of nature does not only find expression in the pilgrimages made at cherry-blossom time *(hanami),* or in the great masses of people who go to the valleys in autumn when the maple trees turn red. It is also evident in a custom which is still very much alive in many areas of Japan — early on a summer morning many people gather by lotus ponds to listen to the blossoms opening up. For most of these people, it is simply a show staged by nature. They come to enjoy the beauty of the unfolding blossoms without thinking of Buddhist ikonography. The lotus symbolizes Buddha. Out of the foul and muddy waters of the pool, a powerful plant grows whose blossoms contain nothing of the mud and dirt below — just like Buddha's enlightenment.

Love of nature in Japan is not only expressed in the enjoyment and care of that which is already present. Nature is also recreated using the means which nature has made available and in accordance with her rules. When entering the Saihôji-Moss-Garden in Kyôto, one has the impression of being in untouched nature. In reality, however, this garden has been laid out with endless care. Over 40 different kinds of moss have been artistically arranged so as to lend a feeling of softness and gentleness to the park. The senses should turn spontaneously towards the manifold shades of green. Blue-green cushions alternate with soft, thick, yellow moss-pillows. In front of the artificial hill, there is a pond, each reflecting the green of the other.

Closeness to nature is found especially in literature. It was a woman, a lady of the court, Murasaki Shikibu, who in the eleventh century wrote the story of Prince Genji. Using a brush she painted over a half-million characters. The story comprises a colourful series of episodes in the life of a nobleman in the *Heian* Period. Hardly a page is without a description of nature. In one scene, nature is plunged in a melancholy mist, in another, the branches of a fir tree are covered with hoar-frost. Flowers and the change of seasons are extolled. Moments of sadness are followed by refreshing scenes of flowers. The poetry of leaves surrounds the life of the handsome prince. Language is also affected by the liveliness of nature. An artist can only express himself in a lively manner when he himself is lively. Inspiration means being alert at a given moment of work.

The importance of nature in architecture can be seen in the story of the Tôshôgû Shrine in Nikkô. This shrine of the 'Sungod coming from the East' is dedicated to the memory of the great General Ieyasu Tokugawa who died in 1616. Twenty years passed before his tomb was completed because, before construction could begin, 40,000 trees had to be transplanted. Today these mighty trees form an impressive cathedral above the buildings of this large complex.

Even the simplest house in Japan has a garden. In Tokyo too, where one can hardly walk between the buildings, each family still finds some small corner for a tiny garden. Often there is only room for a small tree or a bamboo bush, but nature is present, perhaps even more clearly than in an enormous park. The structure of traditional Japanese houses is light. The interior is not separated from the exterior by thick walls. A light breeze blows continually in summer when the sliding doors are pushed back. Often during the warm months of the year, the sliding door to the garden is replaced by a light bamboo curtain. Then, the house is even more a part of the garden, or the garden a part of the house. Even the choice of colours of the walls matches those of nature outside. Loud colours and aggressive patterns are not to be found. A natural colour-scale ranging from fresh green to withered brown is held together by the soft yellow of the tatami matting which covers the floors of the rooms. The effect of Japanese architecture on Europe has already been mentioned. European architecture has, however, also found its own particular way of approaching nature and this in turn helps us to interpret Japan's closeness to nature.

Herbert Read reported on the studies of the Czechoslovakian architect, Karel Honzik, who as early as 1937 pointed out that architecture has not only taken over proportions from the world of plants but has also studied their principles of mechanical construction. In South America, for example, there is a variety of water-lily, *Victoria regia,* whose leaves attain a diameter of two metres and can bear the weight of a child standing on them. The ribs of the leaves have an especially sturdy construction and correspond almost exactly to the roof frame developed by construction engineers for pre-stressed concrete structures. Honzik summarizes, 'Cones, pyramids, parallels, planes and spheres are all constants in nature's engineering. Nature always strives to attain a state of ideal equilibrium between opposing forces. In the moment when this equilibrium has been reached, nature is no longer unstructured. The result for plants, crystals and other natural products is their characteristic form. All living things are constantly in a state of flux; but this movement is governed by universal laws which always strive towards a state of harmony or peace — symmetry, maturity, crystallization. The structure is perfect when the forces have reached a state of equilibrium . . . Human inventions originating in an act of the will strive in the same way towards perfection of form which can only be invalidated through the appearance of new conditions.'

In these thoughts, we find some of the same experiences made by masters of ikebana in the course of generations on the other side of the world. Naturally, Honzik's investigations alone do not lead to an understanding of ikebana. They do, however, contain a presentiment of the Buddhist's concept of world harmony, of the principles of *in* and *yô,* and of the parallels existing between nature and art, i.e. the unity of art and nature.

Closeness to nature in Japan of today is not so much a result of meditation, it has become a vital necessity for many. Polluted air and water, food that is inedible and dangerous to the health, the hectic life in the megalopolis Tokyo, deafening noise and the non-relenting stress of the workaday world, all this would be unbearable had the Japanese not maintained a few refuges of peace and closeness to nature. It is perhaps for this reason that we can explain the great enthusiasm to be found among all classes of Japanese for ikebana. This is documented by the fact that almost 10 per cent of all Japanese are currently enrolled in ikebana courses.

Transitoriness

That transitoriness is regarded as an aesthetic category in Japanese may not at first meet with much understanding among Westerners. Are not stone and bronze the preferred materials of Western sculptors? Haven't the artists of the 'Old World' striven towards being remembered by the coming generations through their works? If art is to be considered a material good, a marketable commodity, or if it is used to demonstrate social or economic special privileges, then the qualities of permanence and age must be considered to be of great value.

Japanese art has never been used as a demonstration of power to the same extent as it has here in the West. Even the palaces of rulers were built in such a way as not to obstruct the natural landscape. Moss-covered cottages in the woods were long valued as retreats by the nobility. Classical Japanese temples are a perfect example of powerlessness. They are built of wood, a non-durable material. The wooden buildings, even the apartment buildings of today, are integrated in the universal waxing and waning of all things.

Ise, Japan's national shrine, is located in the middle of a dark wood. Millions of modern Japanese make a pilgrimage there each year although they no longer literally believe in the myth of the sungoddess Amaterasu as creator of Japan and its people. But the shrine of Ise, more than a thousand years old, enables the Japanese to experience how transitoriness is also a sign of continuity in natural life. The surprisingly simple interior of the shrine, with its archaic design, is made of Hinoki, the wood of Japanese cypresses. The bark of this tree covers the roof. Every 20 years, the building is copied exactly down to the last wooden pin. No-one finds this precise imitation less valuable than original creativity. In this way reverence is expressed for the achievements of their ancestors. After consecrating the new building, the old one is torn down, sawed to pieces, and these pieces are then distributed among the pilgrims.

For the foreigner it is often incomprehensible why the Japanese include living flowers under Ikebana, on the one hand, while, on the other, they daily throw away thousands of tons of withered flowers. Why are rare blossoms removed from plants where, had they been left on, they could have displayed their splendour much longer? Well, it is just the transitoriness of the arrangement and the flowers which lends a special magic to the art of ikebana. This is exactly what makes the creation so valuable. During their short life, the flowers must be handled with special care. And this devotion causes the creator of the composition to forget himself. For one moment at least he experiences the unity of all life. The recognition of the indivisibility of man and his environment *(ninkyô-funi)* is, at such moments, not perceived through the intellect. Nor is it a result of logical argumentation. You, as reader, will certainly experience the differance in these two approaches when you have first of all read this text and then, forgetting everything you have read, devote yourself to the flowers.

Transitoriness means change. Everything is in flux. There is no such thing as the society, the people, or the flower. Every action on the part of man changes the environment. His unhapppiness makes his surroundings unhappy, his laughter brings joy to his environment. Flowers change people, they bring with them feelings of peace, optimism, stillness and the certainty of growth, but also delicacy, naturalness and harmony. People also affect plants. Buddhists call this sympathetic interchange *kannô*.

In the haikus of Matsuo Bashô (1643–1694), we find this play with the transitoriness of life. The other aesthetic categories of Japanese art find an echo here as well. In these haiku poems composed of only seventeen syllables, the idea of transitoriness is expressed without epic breadth. Subtle intimation as in *sabi* expresses much more.

> *Only summer grass*
> *Still remains of all the dreams*
> *Of one-time heroes.*

In the following poem as well, we can experience the power of that which is left unsaid. We see how forcefully growing and withering in nature can be presented in the art of poetry.

> *Perfect quietness.*
> *The song of the cicada*
> *Moves into the rocks.*

The value of things often lies not so much in the things themselves, but rather in the act of reaching out to them, in the relentless procession of life and death. How strong is the suspense that prevails every year in Japan at cherry blossom time. Perhaps the Japanese have developed such devotion to cherry blossoms because their blossoms are of such a short duration. It can also be the intellectual joy of observing the characteristic line of the cherry branch during the course of the year and feeling the shortness of the blossoming period. This has often found expression in Japanese painting. Artists prefer to represent plants in an incomplete state of development. It is the observer who completes the incomplete, and in this way the painting becomes dynamic.

Even the categories of Japanese aesthetics are understood to be in a state of constant change. The history of art is full of ambiguous nuances. Even in the art of flower arrangement, where transitoriness plays a very important role, a change has been making itself felt during the last fifty years. Through the use of durable materials and dried flowers, attempts have been made to make ikebana into 'everlastings'. For modern man stamped by individualism, it has become difficult to invest so much energy into a work of art which he knows has a life expectancy of only a few days. The 'non-floral' arrangement was developed. It suffices to form a piece of sculpture with the sensibility for materials obtained through ikebana, and to call it ikebana although the art work itself is made of granite or iron. For us, however, the limit to what may be called sculpture has been reached. We would only designate as *ikebana* those works of sculpture in which live plants are used. The static aesthetics of the work are not at all of primary concern in ikebana, but rather the aesthetics of the creative art itself.

15

access to ikebana while at the same time protecting him from sliding off into the purely decorative.

When a Japanese speaks of the art of flower arrangement, he merely says *ohana*. This means quite simply 'flower'. The letter 'O' expresses special reverence.

The word that was used to signify flower arrangements was *Shô-ka* which can also be read as *Sei-ka*. The same two ideograms include still a third possible pronunciation: *Ike-bana*. This last pronunciation came into effect in the eighteenth century as the designation for the Japanese art of flower arrangement. The words *Shôka* and *Seika* came to be used to signify earlier styles of ikebana. However, in order to make clear when the entire art of flower arrangement is meant, that is when one has to pronounce *Ikebana,* the Chinese characters are rewritten with letters from the Japanese alphabet: *i, ke, ba* and *na*.

When the Japanese hear the word ikebana, they think first of the flower compositions found in every apartment, in offices and restaurants, of the flowers in season, of the millions of eager ikebana students, of the schools of flower arrangement rich in tradition, or of the rules from the various schools, and they feel ikebana to be an integral part of life. The term ikebana has no élitist overtones, although it was at one time practised by the privileged classes. The actual meaning of the word vibrates with this. The definition of the term may offer to the Westerner a means of

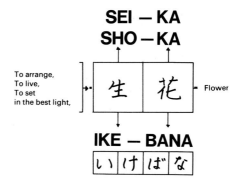

The word is divided into two sections *ike* and *hana* which in this compound is pronounced *-bana*. *Hana* means literally 'flower' in this connection, however, it can be understood as either plant or as part of a plant. *Ike* is derived from three verbs:

ikeru = to place or arrange plants
ikiru = to live, to be alive, to arrive at one's true essence
ikasu = to put in the best light, to help to arrive at its true essence, to make life clearer.

Through the act of arranging flowers in a composition, the life of these flowers becomes more evident. Ikebana is, therefore, not a plastic art form which merely uses plants as 'material'. It is much more than just a question of style, colour and beauty of composition. It is a question of keeping freshness and finding a clear expression of life.

IKEBANA HISTORY

Westerners are continually fascinated by the eventful history of the Japanese art of flower arrangement. Certainly knowing something about historical development of the various ikebana styles can help one to have a better understanding of this art form which is really not at all as esoteric as is often believed.

From Sacrificial Flowers to the Art of Flower Arrangement

The tradition of using flowers as sacrificial objects came to Japan from China by way of Buddhism. Almost 800 years went by before ikebana began, in the fifteenth century, to be cultivated in the homes of the bourgeoisie instead of just in temples and palaces. During this transitional period, in which flowers were used less for sacrificial purposes and more for floral compositions, they also lost their religious significance.

The first form of ikebana was called *Rikka*. At first its function was to portray the Buddhist's Mountain of Recognition, but then increasingly people wanted to use it to represent the beauty and harmony of nature.

Complicated rules of composition prevented this art form from being practised by the common people. It remained a privilege of the nobility and clergy. A new style of ikebana, *Seika* emerged as a counter-movement.

Seika was first generated by the teachings of Zen-Buddhism and then later by those of Confucianism.

Through its rigorous organization, *Seika* expresses the trinity of heaven–man–earth. In this style as well, the masters of ikebana found non-individualistic forms of universal value more desirable than the spontaneous expression of arrogant creativity.

Another new style of ikebana developed from flower arrangements used in the tea ceremony. In this new style, the rigorous formal composition of *Shoka* was no longer visible at first glance. The flowers were thrown into the vase in a natural, relaxed fashion, from which the name *Nagëire* stems. Such compositions are supposed to create a relaxed and cheerful atmosphere.

These three forms have continued to develop side by side and appear today in contemporary style. The end of the last century saw the development of *Moribana,* floral compositions in round, shallow bowls which are so popular today. At that time, plants previously unknown in Japan came into use — tulips, daisies and dahlias. At that time the *kenzan* or needlepoint flower-holder was invented which greatly aided and simplified the technique of flower arrangement.

In the course of ever-increasing foreign influences, many Japanese in the second half of the last century began to look back to traditional Japanese values. Ikebana was introduced as part of the school curriculum.

Soon, art principles originating in other cultures began to influence the art of flower arrangement. Plastics and metals, even scrap, are used today to create contrast to the flowers. Since 1950 Ikebana has become an increasingly international art form.

The following diagrams show in simplified form the development of the individual Ikebana styles. The diagrams should also demonstrate, however, that all these forms are contemporary in style and very lively. We are conscious of the fact that a summary of the development of Ikebana leaves a good deal unsaid about many tendencies which from a historical point of view are much more complicated than we are able to show here in our diagrams.

RIKKA

The word Rikka, also known as *Tatebana,* means either 'standing flowers' or 'luxurious bouquet'.

HISTORY	FORM

6th — 14th centuries

Period of Sacrificial Flowers
bukka (flowers for Buddha).

Arranged by priests as part of ceremony in temple.

Mainly blossoms, buds and leaves of the lotus, placed usually in an upright position in a narrow-necked vase. Flowers are also presented in sacrificial baskets *(kero)* and shallow bowls.

12th — 14th centuries

Pre-Rikka Period
The *Mitsugusoku* (three things on a table) develops as a decoration for the newly developed tatami-rooms in temples and palaces.
Earliest rules of composition for this are in *Kadensho* by Mon-ami (1131).

Usually three objects arranged on a flat table:

1. Flower arrangement already similar to that of Rikka.
2. Torch-holder.
3. Incense vessel with incense box and fire-making implement.

14th — 16th centuries

Rikka Formation Period
New style in home construction provides for a niche of honour *(tokonoma)*.

Rikka practised by priests, members of nobility and samurai.

Stronghold of flower arrangement: Rokkakudô Temple, Kyôto (Ikenobô School).

A straight upright form growing out of a slender base (shin style of Rikka).

Especially in bronze vases or opulent Chinese and Korean porcelain containers.

立華

EXAMPLES

MEANING

Sacrificial flower *(bukka)*.

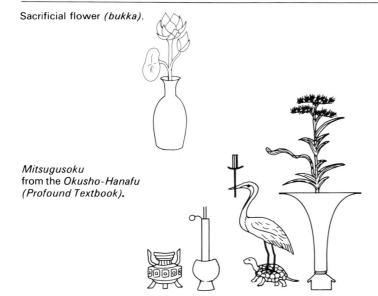

Offering to Buddha.
Expression of love of nature and of the divine in nature.
Lotus symbolizes purity and Buddha.
Ceremony performed in honour of Buddha.

Mitsugusoku
from the *Okusho-Hanafu*
(Profound Textbook).

Presented in a temple or home of a nobleman in honour of the visit of a member of the royal family.
Upright centre branch already signifies 'truth'.
Incense and light used to enhance presentation.

Truth *(Shin)* dominates in this composition.
Representation of world system.
All parts have symbolic names: knowledge, honour, prudence, charity, assistance, sacrifice, river, etc.

Recorded by
Ikenobô Senkô I (1562)
in the *Okusho-Rikka-Hiden*
(Rikka Secret Textbook).

Rikka Formation Period — continued.

Lively, inclined style: *Nokijin* style.

Also arranged mainly in bronze vases.

15th — 18th centuries

Golden Age of Rikka

Ikebana becomes an art form in its own right.

Style becomes broader, softer.

Famous Ikenobô masters at the courts.

Suna-no-mono ('sand things') placed in sand-filled wooden or bronze basins.

Oldest Rikka textbook: *Sendenshô* (1445).

Composition contains seven or nine main elements.

Flower competitions and exhibitions in palaces.

Rare, colourful plants are preferred.

Wealthy citizens as well cultivate Ikebana especially on the occasion of feasts and celebrations.

Colourful.

18th — 19th centuries

Period of Formal Rikka

Merchants, citizens, nobility and priests practise this art.

Exact imitations of traditional models.

New schools come into being.

Nine main elements.

Odd, bizarre plant forms are preferred.

EXAMPLES	MEANING

Nokijin-Rikka
by Ikenobô Senkô (1587)
from the book
Ikenobô-Senkô-Rikka-Fu.

The human heart *(Shin)* and nature are always in motion.

Landscape of the mythical mountain is used to symbolize the world.

Rikka, Suna-no-mono by Master Daijô-in, published in 1678 in *Suna-no-mono Textbook.*

Search for new styles.

The 'truth' *(Shin)* becomes dynamic.

Religious content becomes less important.

Representation of a landscape by the sea.

Expression of beauty and harmony in nature.

Idealistic view of world

Demonstration of wealth.

Rikka by Ikenobô-Sen-i from the book *Suna-no-mono-zu* (1761).

Emphasis placed on external form and technical perfection.

Man tries to strengthen himself by overcoming technical problems of composition.

Reflections on value of Japanese history.

21

20th century

Rikka Modern Period

Ikebana becomes popular among all classes in Japan.

Worldwide diffusion.

1958 revival of Rikka by Ikenobô.

Rikka in modern apartments, in entrance ways of public buildings and for celebrations.

Exhibitions all over the world.

1. Classical Rikka:

   Traditional combination of materials.

   Use of classical containers.

   Principles of composition and technique as in Rikka of classical period from fifteenth to nineteenth centuries.

2. Modern Rikka:

   A freer combination of plants.

   Simplified styles.

   Small Rikka for home and office.

   Use of kenzan (needlepoint holder).

3. Creative Rikka:

   Very free style but still rising up from one point.

   Use of new materials like metal, plastic, etc.

   Freer use of methods employed in the plastic arts such as colour, mass, line, surfaces and emptiness in creating a theme.

   Arrangements made of non-floral materials make connection with abstract sculpture.

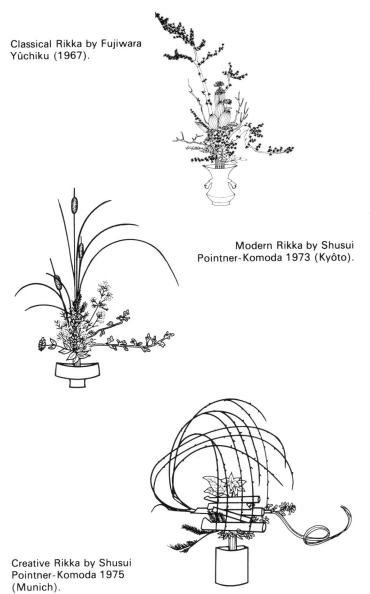

Classical Rikka by Fujiwara
Yûchiku (1967).

Complicated rules of composition are observed in order
to increase concentration and sensibility.

Modern Rikka by Shusui
Pointner-Komoda 1973 (Kyôto).

Expression of the desire for order and harmony in the
world.

Representation of universal values in nature.

Desire for peace.

Personal expression of the artist.

A theme is stated in an original manner from the fields
of technology, natural science, politics, philosophy, etc.

Creative Rikka by Shusui
Pointner-Komoda 1975
(Munich).

SHÔKA
SEIKA

This word means 'placid living flowers'. A Seika is simpler than a Rikka, however, and it rises up from a point. The character for *Seika* can also be read *Shôka*.

HISTORY	FORM

15th — 17th centuries

Preparation Period of Seika

Under the influence of Zen-Buddhism *Chabana* emerges (flower arrangement for the tea ceremony).

Promoted by the influential counsellors for art and culture at the courts *(dôhôshû)*.

Practised by nobles and intellectuals.

As compared to Rikka very simple, small and natural.

Often only one flower is used.

Gives the feeling of improvisation.

Only a few rules.

Simple, modest containers of bamboo or matt-glazed ceramic.

17th century

Formation Period of Seika

Many textbooks are written.

Period of *Sashibana* (also read *Sôka,* arranged flowers).

Tsuribana as house decoration.

Seika or Shôka are considered as alternatives to the more complicated Rikka.

Two to three lines emerging from base.

A simple vase.

Hanging containers in shape of a moon or ship made out of copper or bamboo are preferred.

For Seika, vases, bowls and cups are used.

Looser compositions.

No ceremonial effect.

Arrangements are quite small and well suited for modest homes.

EXAMPLES

MEANING

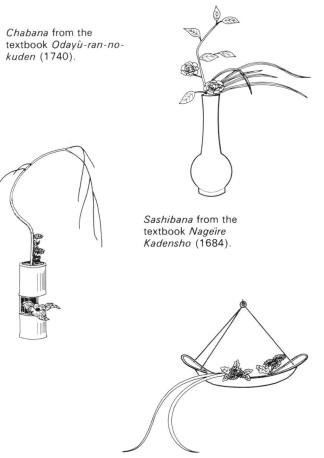

Chabana from the textbook *Odayû-ran-no-kuden* (1740).

Sashibana from the textbook *Nageïre Kadensho* (1684).

Seika hanging flower lamp from the textbook *Kodai-seika-zukan* (1710).

'Simple heart' stillness, simplicity 'poverty' (Jap.: *wabi, sabi*).

Improve the atmosphere between people in a room.

Silent welcome or farewell greeting.

One line is for the guest, the other for the host, together they build a harmonious unity.

Natural simplicity.

Joyful calmness.

Symbolism of the ship (life's journey, arrival, departure, loaded ships, etc.).

Joy of watching the moon.

Symbolism of plants (i.e. pine tree means long life).

18th — 19th centuries

Golden Age of Shôka

Under Ikenobô Senjô, in 1816, the rules of classical Shôka were laid down and are still valid today.

Wealthy citizens and intellectuals devote themselves to Shôka.

Since 1888 ikebana has been part of the school curriculum for girls.

Means of reflecting on Japanese culture at a time of revolutionary influences from abroad.

Three lines emerge from base line.

Various nomenclatures.

Mostly *Shin, Soe, Tai* or *Shin, Soe, Hikae*.

Precise rules are set concerning containers and materials.

Strict arrangement.

Usually one or two kinds of plants are used.

Increasing rigidity.

20th century

Modern Period of Shôka

Ikebana has never been so popular as in this century.

Like in classical music, classical Shôka along with Shôka in modern style are practised.

Formation of modern Shôka.

Rules laid down in 1854 by the Ikenobô Academy *(Shôka-Sanshuike)*.

Shinputai, tracing back to the very simple beginnings of Shôka, is developed by Headmaster Ikenobô Senei since 1977.

1. Classical Shôka:
   Rather strict, but noble and simple in arrangement.

2. Shôka-Sanshuike (Shôka made of three materials) the form is rounder, fuller and livelier; colour combinations, contrast and character of plants are significant.

3. Shinputai uses only very few selected materials; rises from one base.

Seika arrangement with aspidistra leaves from the textbook *Tokiwa-Kagami* (1852).

Classical *Shôka* arrangement in traditional bronze container.

Modern *Shôka* with European plants (spindle tree branches, gladiola leaves, dahlia) by Shusui Pointner-Komoda (1971).

Individual expression should be avoided in favour of non-individualistic forms.

Expression of the system in nature.

Trinity of heaven, man and earth, or of positive, negative and human being.

Strict rules.

In some schools, the Shin branch is regarded as representing the emperor.

A counter-movement to this is the *Bunjin-bana,* the freer unconventional Ikebana of the man of letters.

Absorption in classical art leads to harmony and inner peace.

Often a theme serves as the point of departure for the composition.

A title can clarify the intention of the artist.

The individuality of the artist is permitted to make itself felt through the non-individualistic form.

Harmony between the character of the plants and the intention of the artist is the important meaning of Shinputai.

NAGEÏRE
HEIKA

Nageïre means 'flowers thrown into' and can also be read *Heika*. Tall vases are usually employed.

HISTORY	FORM
15th — 16th centuries	
Preparatory Period of Nageïre	Simple, quite small, natural.
Flowers for the tea ceremony *(Chabana)*.	Flowers give impression of being casually thrown into the vase.
Influenced by Zen-Buddhism.	Hardly any rules.
Practised by nobles and intellectuals.	Often only one flower is used.
17th — 19th centuries	
Period of Nageïrebana	Usually two lines in an unconstrained arrangement.
Contemporary with Golden Age of Rikka.	The receptacles are not so luxurious as in Rikka.
Shôka comes into being at this time.	Clear, noble lines are stressed.
Nobles and educated classes seek simplicity.	In addition to Rikka and Shôka which became increasingly formalized, Nageïre remains quite an informal composition.
	Simpler, usually three-group construction.
20th century	
Golden Age of Nageïre	In all schools it comprises three main lines.
Europe and the West exert an influence on some Ikebana masters.	Arrangements in vases of all kinds: ceramic, glass, porcelain, etc.
Becomes known internationally.	

EXAMPLES

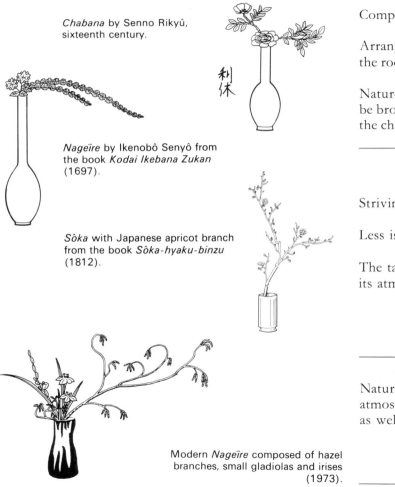

Chabana by Senno Rikyû, sixteenth century.

Nageïre by Ikenobô Senyô from the book *Kodai Ikebana Zukan* (1697).

Sôka with Japanese apricot branch from the book *Sôka-hyaku-binzu* (1812).

Modern *Nageïre* composed of hazel branches, small gladiolas and irises (1973).

MEANING

Completion of tea ceremony.

Arrangement should be effective but should not dominate the room.

Nature's seasonal appearance should, in condensed form, be brought into the interior of the tea house by means of the chabana.

Striving for naturalness.

Less is more.

The task of Nageïre is to bring something of nature and its atmosphere into the ever-growing cities.

Natural features of the plant used should determine the atmosphere and character of the arrangement — today as well.

MORIBANA

Moribana means literally 'piled up flowers'.

HISTORY	FORM

End of the 19th century

Early Period of Moribana	Natural arrangement in shallow bowls.
Numerous ikebana masters develop a free landscape arrangement generally using *Rikka Sunanomono* (sand arrangement) as point of departure.	Use of foreign flowers (tulips, daisies, dahlias).
	The three main lines form an irregular triangle.
Rules are set by Ohara Unshin (about 1900).	Invention of the needlepoint holder *(kenzan)* enables everyone to realize simple Ikebana arrangements quickly.

Golden Age of Moribana 20th century	Technically simple.
Very popular style of ikebana.	Can be made very quickly.
Finds acceptance in all levels of society due to its simplicity.	Branches, leaves, flowers are arranged in shallow bowls, cups and chalices.
After 1945 internationally known.	Unlike Rikka, Shôka or Nageïre, designed for an all-round view.
Influence of foreign principles of art.	Table arrangements are to be observed from all sides *(Shimentai).*
Jiyû-ka, 'the free style', comes into being.	

Beginning at about 1930

Avant-garde Ikebana (Zenei-ka)	In addition to fresh and dried plants of all kinds, stones, metals and plastics are used to form sculptures.
Strongly supported by Teshigahara Sôfu.	
The boundary between abstract sculpture and Ikebana becomes blurred in 'non-floral' compositions.	Sculptures made out of roots, without container.

EXAMPLES

MEANING

Simple, unpretentious *Moribana* by Ohara Unshin (approximately 1909).

A miniature cosmos should be brought into the home.

Miniature landscape.

Representation of the seasons.

Moribana symbolizes freedom, worldliness and peace.

The principle of heaven–man–earth is interpreted in various manners by the various Ikebana schools. Sometimes the highest branch represents heaven, or in the Oriental-Buddhist sense, man or Shin is the most important element.

Moribana by Shusui Pointner-Komoda (1971).

Expression of joy about nature.

An idea is expressed artistically.

The intention of the artist can sometimes be made clearer by using a title.

To some extent an emphasis on purely decorative element.

Man expresses certain ideas and feelings through the use of natural floral or artificial lines, colours and masses in free combinations.

A wider field for experimentation opens up to the artist in the direction of sculpture.

Ikebana, free style by Shusui Pointner-Komoda (1972).

Important elements in Ikebana which distinguish it from other plastic art forms are abandoned by some schools.

31

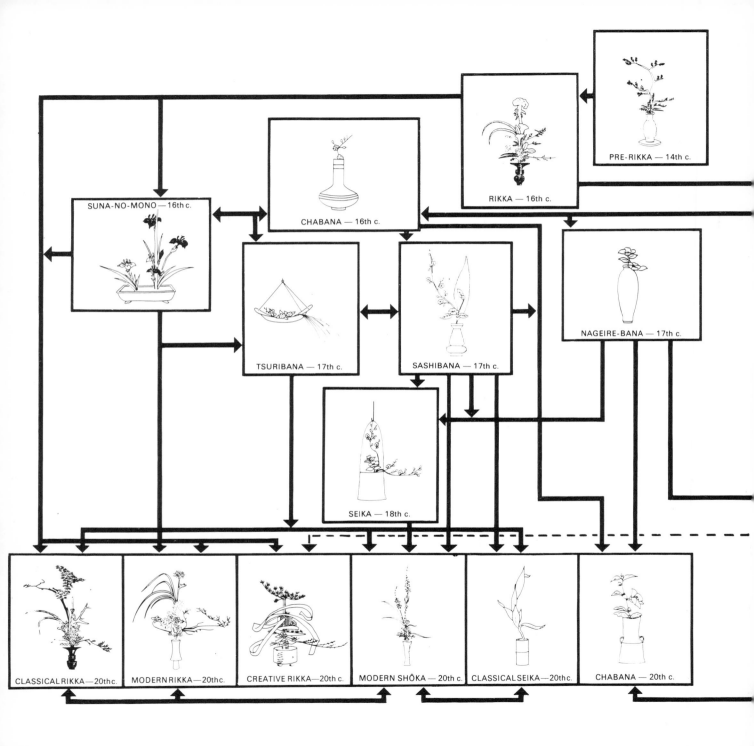

PRE-RIKKA — 14th c.

RIKKA — 16th c.

SUNA-NO-MONO — 16th c.

CHABANA — 16th c.

NAGEIRE-BANA — 17th c.

TSURIBANA — 17th c.

SASHIBANA — 17th c.

SEIKA — 18th c.

CLASSICAL RIKKA — 20th c.

MODERN RIKKA — 20th c.

CREATIVE RIKKA — 20th c.

MODERN SHÔKA — 20th c.

CLASSICAL SEIKA — 20th c.

CHABANA — 20th c.

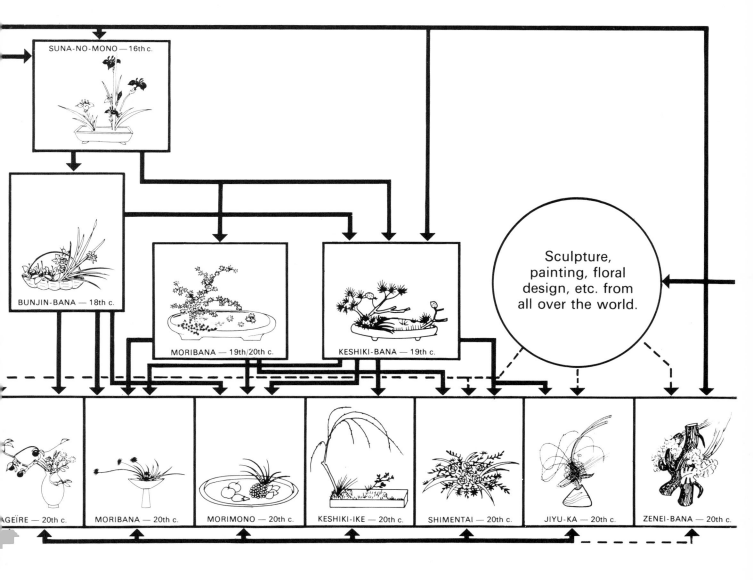

SUNA-NO-MONO — 16th c.

BUNJIN-BANA — 18th c.

MORIBANA — 19th/20th c.

KESHIKI-BANA — 19th c.

Sculpture, painting, floral design, etc. from all over the world.

AGEÏRE — 20th c.

MORIBANA — 20th c.

MORIMONO — 20th c.

KESHIKI-IKE — 20th c.

SHIMENTAI — 20th c.

JIYU-KA — 20th c.

ZENEI-BANA — 20th c.

IKEBANA TODAY

Due to a rather large number of publications available in the West dealing with ikebana, readers may get the impression that Ikebana refers exclusively to flower arrangements in *shallow bowls*. But ikebana is like music as, here too, one can be satisfied with something as simple as a pastoral wooden flute.

The first notes played on this instrument might also be regarded as the beginning of a life with, and for, music. No-one would deny the fact that in order to be able to interpret the master works of classical music, one has first to master the rules of harmony, and the technique of playing. A musician could hardly be called such, if he were unable to play an instrument or read notes, nor if he rejected all musical traditions. At best, he would only be able to make sounds or noise, but these could not be called music according to the prevailing world consensus.

Since the basic materials employed in ikebana are flowers and plants which are beautiful themselves, it is sometimes difficult to distinguish the *noise* from the *music*. On the other hand, however, since flowers are beautiful, everyone has the chance of creating beautiful compositions right from the start.

The illustrations on pages 32/33 demonstrate three things:

1. Ikebana is not static. Ikebana does not mean copying art forms of times long past. Ikebana has always been progressive and dynamic despite its strong sense of tradition. Even nature, the yardstick, has not remained the same, since it too is subject to the dynamics of change and development.

2. Today's ikebana is firmly anchored in the traditions of Japanese art. It does, however, assimilate foreign influences as well. Rikka is the root from which all other styles have developed whether directly or indirectly.

3. In the course of its long history, ikebana has never exhibited more possibilities than today. Today everything is possible from esoteric compositions based entirely on a Buddhistic–Confucianistic tradition to superficial works of sculpture wavering between decoration and pure effect.

The individual periods of Japanese flower arrangements are made clear by means of illustrations of typical styles of that period. The continual transitions and the many undercurrents influencing the various directions, as well as the numerous possibilities offered by modern ikebana can only be suggested here. We should also like to note that investigations into the history of ikebana still have not been able to show such clear-cut results as might be suggested by the simplified review presented.

PATHS TOWARDS TRUTH

The search for truth is an essential part of the essence of art. But what is truth? It is certainly connected with perfection and accomplishment, with liveliness, with correctness and wholeness. Opinions vary as to how this end is to be attained. For some, the only way is through the power of the intellect and the rules of logic. Planning and discarding, analysing and synthesizing, comparing and measuring are necessary for this approach. But direct experience and perception of truth in modern life have less importance. This is also the problem of this book. Naturally, we have to explain and present our arguments so as to introduce the reader to the spirit and technique of ikebana. We are convinced, however, that the real spirit of ikebana cannot be made understandable through words. Therefore, you, the reader, should first of all look at the pictures. You should choose flowers and bring them into your home. You should enjoy the beauty of the natural world.

Japanese traditional arts as 'paths'

If art is supposed to lead to truth, then it is not to be perceived with the intellect alone, but with the feelings as well. Artist and observer are challenged as whole persons. Only the whole person can experience truth. We can perhaps recognize that art offers a path even without a knowledge of Zen-Buddhism, if we assume that art strives towards truth.

The various artistic disciplines in Japan have long been understood as paths, although *do* (path) cannot be strictly defined. Today, the Japanese perceives these paths to be independent of religion, despite the fact that religion provided their origin. Boddhidharma is considered the twenty-eighth patriarch of Buddhism. He believed that the true teachings of Buddha could not be learned from a book because truth is too deep to be expressed in words. Quiet meditation, and directionless lingering were for him the means of attaining enlightenment.

Inner composure is not gained only by meditation while sitting or walking, however. Under the influence of Zen-Buddhism which traces its origins to Boddhidharma, the Japanese arts became so spiritualized that they too were regarded as *do*. The creative act became more important than the resulting creation itself. Working harmoniously became important. The creative person looked for harmony in his relations to society and nature. Perfection can be attained by taking one of these paths. It is not always easy for the Westerner to understand that the Japanese consider fencing an art. In this physical art form, the Japanese recognize another path leading to self-fulfilment. The advanced participant of this discipline is able to forget himself. He no longer has the feeling that he carries out the action of striking but rather that the action completes itself. Just as here in *Ken-dô,* so it is in *Kyû-dô,* the art of archery. All over the world *Jû-dô* leads to a spirit of sportmanship and self-discipline. There are also other methods which help one return to the source of his own being: *Sho-dô,* the art of calligraphy, *Sa-dô,* the art of preparing tea, usually referred to as the tea ceremony, and finally, the art of flower arrangement, *Ka-dô* — the flower path.

Ka-dô, the flower path

Of course the 'path-character' of the Japanese art of flower arrangement cannot be experienced through this book alone. This book should serve to inspire our readers to set out on this path. He who has worked his way attentively through the lessons offered, he who has composed each of the arrangements in each season and with various plants will be able to bear witness to the fact that the various paths leading to ikebana are independent of religious convictions.

When arranging flowers, the first thing we take into consideration is the natural growth pattern of the flowers and branches. Only then can we bring this natural growth line and our idea of composition into harmony with each other. This creative act can lead to a state of inner composure. But this 'inward communication' *(sanmai)* should not be disturbed by awkwardness in the handling of delicate blossoms or difficulties encountered when fixing branches in a vase. The techniques of arranging flowers must be so perfectly mastered that each individual movement of the hands is made without conscious effort.

He who has attained this will begin to feel the power of the 'flower path'. He will experience how his bodily movements, his facial expressions, and the movements of his hands adapt themselves to the character of the flower he is handling. A pine branch demands different treatment than a delicate blade of grass.

Ikebana teachers note a change in their students' attitudes. Through the non-directional arranging of flowers many become calmer and mentally more well-balanced. Their ability to withstand psychological pressure increases which means that they are better able to stand up to the pressures of modern daily life. Working continually with living flowers causes something of the essence of the plants to rub off on the persons working with them. Calmness is attained, sensitivity increases and one becomes peaceful. How very powerful is the life force of plants even without noise or haste. Silence takes on value. When even in other areas of life the essence of flowers determines one's actions, the Japanese speak of having attained 'flower hearts' (*hananokokoro*).

We do not wish to maintain that enlightenment will be reached by everyone who has chosen the way of the flowers, but most Westerners will find the way to greater inner harmony through ikebana, and sometimes they will be very happy without being able to say exactly why.

APPROACHING IKEBANA THROUGH ONE'S OWN CREATIONS

Speaking about and reading books about the art of flower arrangement cannot afford one the essential experience needed. It is, first of all, the love of flowers which makes ikebana more than just the creation of artistic forms. Living flower compositions remain fresh for only a few days. They are not a marketable commodity. Ikebana, unlike the decorative, transportable European bouquet, cannot be made a piece of merchandise. In ikebana the end product is not of primary importance. Harmony of composition arises by itself when the artist is in harmony with tradition and nature. A glance at the other typically Japanese arts illustrates the fact that the creative act itself is more important than the thing created.

Let us take for example the 'tea-path' *(Sa-dô)*. Its secret lies simply in the fact that tea is prepared and drunk in harmony with the guest and the surroundings. Every movement of the hands while preparing the tea becomes a work of art, each movement affects the person performing the ceremony, the guest and the tea as well.

Through the repeated act of *ikeru*, attitudes towards plants develop. The quiet observation of nature and the physical communication with flowers often lead to inner equilibrium, peace, serenity and increased concentration. While practising ikebana, one only thinks of the flowers. He who works superficially or hectically will soon discover that the flowers wither more quickly. A completely free use of tones and noises, of sounds and words, of colours, forms and movements surely leads to chaos. Every art form, every artist and even the so-called 'layman' is bound by certain traditions. Even if he tries to free himself from these traditions with all his might, they continue to influence him. His creation is stamped with the attitudes of his time, of his society, and of the school to which he belongs. Even the greatest masters did not work in a vacuum, but they did leave behind a world which had not existed before them. With this observation we want to show how valuable the Japanese method of learning is. The creative process begins with imitating the master. The use of ever new materials prevents mindless copying.

This book is not meant to replace the teacher. But in those cases where a master is not available it can help the learner to come a few steps further along the 'way of flowers'. A rich array of model arrangements in simple and complicated compositions invite you to recreate them. Criticism should be set aside until a free play with the styles offered has been attained, and until the flowers and plants of each season can be combined harmoniously in these styles.

THE TECHNIQUE OF
IKEBANA

IKEBANA FORMS AND STYLES

Moribana

Upright style	A	
	B	
	C	
Slanting style	A	
	B	
	C	
Hanging style	A	
	B	
	C	

Variations of basic styles
Combinations of different styles
Morimono (arrangement of fruits and vegetables in shallow bowls)
Keshiki-ike (landscape arrangements)
Futakabu-ike (two-group Moribana)

Nageïre (Heika)

Upright style	A	
	B	
	C	
Slanting style	A	
	B	
	C	
Hanging style	A	
	B	
	C	

Variations of basic styles
Combinations of different styles
Futakabu-ike (two-group Nageïre)

Shôka (Seika)

Classical Shôka	Shin-style
	Gyô-style
	Sô-style
Modern Shôka	Shin-style
	Gyô-style
	Sô-style
Shinputai	

Rikka

Classical Rikka	(Styles: see page 156)
Modern Rikka	Sugushin (Shin is vertical)
	Noki-jin (Shin is lively)
	Sunanomono (Rikka in sand basin)

Free Style

With container
Without container
Floral arrangement
Non-floral arrangement
Zenei-bana (avant-garde arrangement)

Now that we have read about different ways of approaching ikebana which can help us to understand the art and the far-away world from which it comes, we should like to prepare for the practical exercises.

The lessons have been prepared and tested in accordance with the knowledge and skills we assume a European or non-Japanese can bring to the art of ikebana. We have taken care that the flowers and branches used in these lessons are available here in our natural surroundings, in gardens, flower shops and nurseries.

Each lesson has been arranged in such a way as to proceed from the simple to the more advanced. We shall begin with Moribana and then work our way through Nageïre and Shôka to Rikka.

We have purposely left the treatment of free styles to last because we believe that free creativity is only of value when the technical side has been mastered, experience gained and personal tastes and attitudes acquired.

The variety of main forms and styles available in Ikebana are shown in the accompanying list.

About courses and lessons

The simple style of Moribana will serve as an introduction to the Japanese art of flower arrangement. This approach has proved itself on many occasions. Advanced students of ikebana are advised to refresh their knowledge by repeating from time to time all Moribana compositions before trying their hand at Nageïre. Only after enough self-confidence has been acquired should one go on to deal with Shôka. Rikka, due to its many lines and strict requirements concerning a feeling for the material, should only be practised after completion of the first three courses. Thereafter, one can try one's hand at free creation. Hands and spirit are now ready for free creative expression. This should by no means be misunderstood because, in Moribana, creative powers are trained and needed. The sequence in which the individual lessons should be worked through depends upon the flowers and branches available to the student. It would be senseless to force the upward growing branches of a pine tree into a hanging Nageire composition simply to follow the sequence offered in the book. One shouldn't be afraid to practise the upright style once again, this time with other branches and suitable flowers.

Practising with other plants

Ideally, the student should arrange all the styles shown with all possible plants for each of the four seasons. In this way he could, on one occasion, use flowers, leaves and branches which are similar to those used in our lessons, and then another time, those which are completely different in character.

Each time new material comes into play, creative ability is called for in spite of the prescribed style. Anyone who tries his hand at ikebana and stays with it for a while will notice that flower arranging is not simply a rigid sticking to the rules and regulations, that no composition is exactly like another one, and that each new one demands a certain amount of creativity. Those who live on moorland will discover new plants when visiting the mountains or seashore and these will serve to inspire new compositions. Even the same kind of plants look different in the flat lands than in the mountains. Flowers growing in dry regions look different from those in moorlands and river banks. This is why no-one will ever compose the same ikebana twice.

Collect plants

Those studying ikebana and following the lessons in this book will have new experiences as well. They will start to go on hikes again, they will leave the car behind and follow a path through the woods. They will also realize that they suddenly see plants in a different light, that plants which they did not even notice before now catch their attention. All at once they will discover lines and patterns in the trees that they had never noticed before and they will be aware of different shades of green. In short, their relationship to plants will have changed. They will no longer carry bulky bouquets of indiscriminately picked flowers but, rather, just a few carefully chosen flowers and well-matched branches. Delicate grasses and weather-beaten roots take on new meaning.

Take your time

Ikebana needs time. Impatience and haste should be set aside when dealing with flowers. A flower arrangement, as it is understood in ikebana, cannot be started today and then perhaps be completed next week.

The peculiarities of the flowers demand that one stick to it until the ikebana composition has been completed. Interruptions and continual changes of location and lighting have an adverse effect on the flowers.

Meditation

We would like to use the word meditation without pathos. Meditation takes place when we are quiet like the plants themselves, and when we touch and arrange them. After having studied the illustrations and directions offered, the student of ikebana should try to exclude the intellect. He should not wish to play with the plants but rather he should try to live with them, forming them into a living artistic creation. Within a short time he will have gained peace and emotional balance through dealing with plants. He relaxes, he breathes more easily and he gains a feeling for the plants in his hands and enjoys their fragrance.

Each lapse of concentration is registered by the flowers: stems bend, branches break and blossom petals fall off too soon. Through the practice of ikebana everyone can feel that genuine artistic expression has its genesis in meditation and that art leads back to meditation, to communication with the work of art itself.

The diagrams

In many lessons you will find illustrations which simplify the main sections or lines of the composition. In order to show clearly the direction of the branches and other parts of the plants, most of the flower arrangements are shown both from the front and from the top. The front elevation shows the inclination of the various elements to the horizontal, while the plan view gives the position of all the items relative to one another.

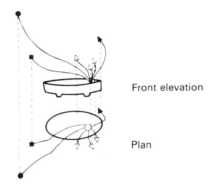

Front elevation

Plan

Notes

As a reminder, ikebana students should make a sketch of each of their arrangements. A sketch is more effective than a photograph for close observation of flowers, leaves, proportions and contrasts within the composition.

Tools for the beginner

1 **Scissors.** The best are a pair of special Ikebana scissors. They have two razor-sharp cutting edges. Garden shears are well suited to cutting branches and twigs but are not particularly good for delicate flowers and thin leaf stems because they press too hard on the veins of the plants. A sharp knife can be used instead. For detail work its sharp point comes in handy as well.

2 **Handsaw.** A small all-purpose handsaw is very useful for cutting thick branches and twigs.

3 **A soft piece of cloth.** The cloth serves to keep the work space clean. It also helps keep down noise if you place the scissors on it instead of on the table top. It can also be used to cover plants when the cut-point has to be singed.

4 **Water container.** Water is kept in this small bowl while working on the arrangement. The stems can be cut under water in this bowl so as not to dirty the water in the ikebana container.

5 **Kenzan.** It is a good idea to obtain a rather large flower holder (*kenzan,* needlepoint holder) right at the outset as this is less likely to be tipped over by full arrangements than a narrower holder. The base of the kenzan should be as heavy as possible (lead-antimony).

6 **Kenzan-naoshi.** The *kenzan-naoshi* is a small, useful object used to straighten out the needles of the kenzan and to clean between them.

7 **Flower wire.** Wire in several different widths is needed. Even more useful is wire with a green coating.

8 **Bast.** In certain arrangements bast can replace the wire and has the advantage of not rusting.

9 **Florist's tape.** This self-adhesive, waterproof plastic tape (green or brown) is very handy.

10 **Pebbles or glass beads.** They serve to hold down or cover up the kenzan.

IKEBANA LESSONS

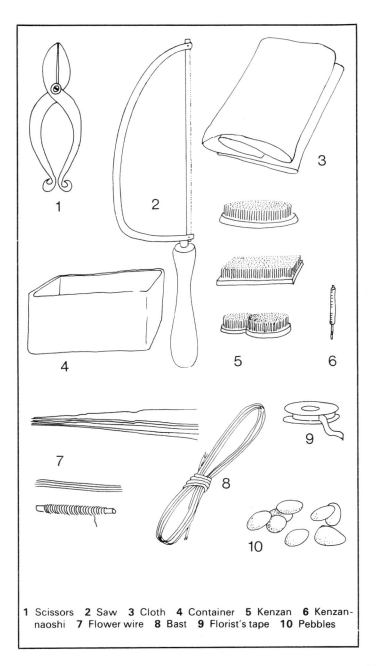

1 Scissors 2 Saw 3 Cloth 4 Container 5 Kenzan 6 Kenzan-naoshi 7 Flower wire 8 Bast 9 Florist's tape 10 Pebbles

MORIBANA

What does Moribana mean?

Moribana literally means 'flowers arranged in a mass effect' and implies a rather free, quite natural flower arrangement. The translation 'flower bush' perhaps best conveys the essence of Moribana.

moru — | MORI | BANA | — **hana**

(to pile something on a container)

(flower, blossom)

The master flower arranger and founder of the Ohara School developed this style at the turn of the century from various traditional arrangements. He simplified their strict rules adapting them to the needs of the times. Ideas borrowed from the Sunano-mono-Rikka are evident in Moribana. Suiriku-ike, the land-water-arrangement and Gyodo-ike, the fish-way-arrangement are two examples of the two-group Shôka style which have very obviously influenced this new form. Moribana offers the beginner easy access to the art of flower arrangement.

Moribana is an ikebana style usually arranged in a bowl or cup. Most often the *kenzan* (needlepoint holder) serves as the flower holder, less often another kind of flower holder called the *shippo* is used.

How is the needlepoint holder used?

1. Very thin branches or flower stems cannot be stuck onto the points of the the needlepoint holder. Therefore, a piece of another branch or a small piece of wood is bound to the branch or stem by means of a thin piece of flower-wire or florist's tape.
2. Blossom stems and grass can easily be made thicker by winding a piece of paper around the ends.
3. Very thin stems can be introduced into the stems or other flowers or branches provided these are hollow, fleshy or filled with pith.

4. When branches lean heavily in one direction causing the kenzan to topple, another needlepoint holder can prevent this by weighing down the first.
5. Branches are usually cut on a slant, then placed vertically onto the kenzan. Only then are they bent in the desired direction.

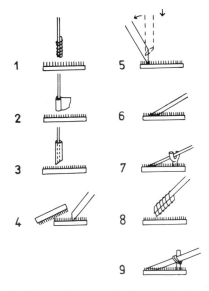

Methods of fastening stems in the needlepoint holder

6. Very soft branches can be fixed onto the kenzan by the cut edge.
7. If straight branches are to slant at a low angle in one direction a small supporting twig can be used to hold them in place.
8. If a heavy branch is to slant at a low angle, the base can be strengthened by binding another piece of branch to the bottom, this enables the branch to be supoported by several needles.
9. Here, a branch projecting far out is supported by a small piece of wood using the method described in 7.

MORIBANA

KENZAN AND CONTAINERS

1 Straightening the needles with the kenzan-naoshi
2 Kenzan, kenzan-naoshi, and slip prevention mat made of rubber for kenzan
3, 4, 12, 13, 14, 15, 17. Ceramic bowls
5 Glass bowl
6, 7, 8, 18. Ceramic cups
11, 12. Bowls made of wood and bamboo
9 Moon-shaped container
16 Iron bowl with feet
19 Combination containers

	3
1	4
2	5

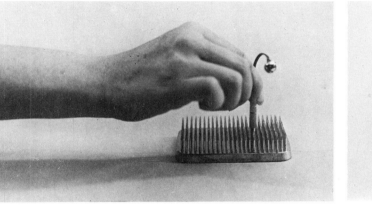

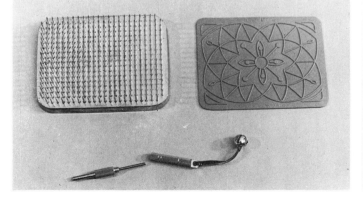

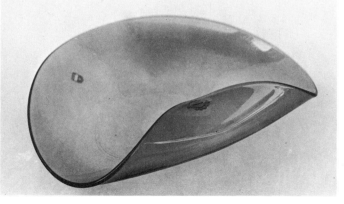

43

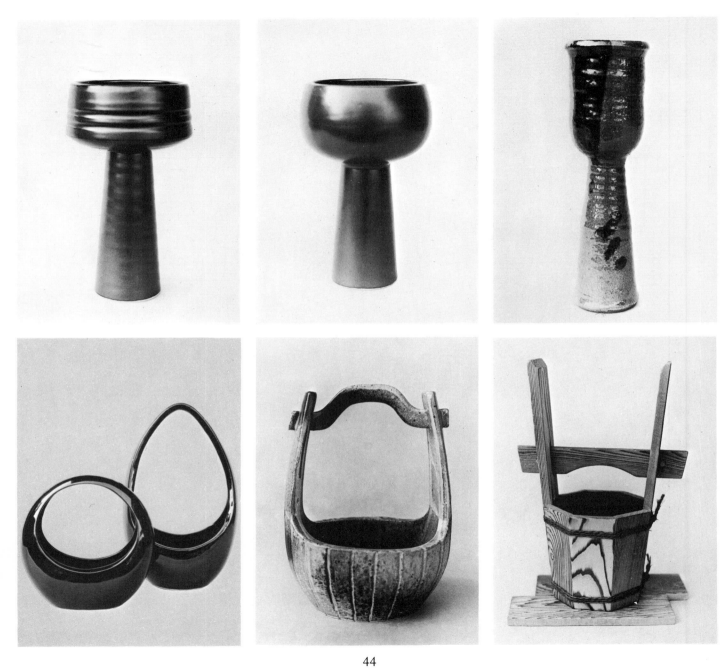

Which containers are most suitable for Moribana arrangements?

Beginners need at first a simple, shallow bowl. It can be round or rectangular, oval or square. Size, colour and material should be chosen to suit the surroundings in which the arrangement is to be displayed, as well as the kind of flowers and branches used. In the beginning, solid colour containers are preferable to colourful or patterned ones. It is important that the sides of the container be at least 4 cm in height, otherwise the flower holder will not be totally submerged beneath the surface of the water.

Many kinds of bowls and cups made of ceramic, porcelain, metal, glass or plastic are suitable for Moribana arrangements. Even small baskets in which a ceramic container has been placed are good especially for delicate summer compositions.

What are the component parts of Moribana?

Moribana, Nageïre and Shôka always comprise three main parts. The various schools are all in agreement on this point. The expression 'main parts' is more apt than 'main lines' because sometimes these elements are composed of leafy surfaces or masses of blossoms and leaves bound together rather than lines. The three main parts together with their end points (blossoms) or focal points form an irregular triangle, the surface of which should be neither vertical nor horizontal. Please check your compositions on this point, for we have discovered that many flower arrangements here in the West tend to be very flat without spatial effect. This can be traced to the fact that many non-Japanese have learned Ikebana from books in which the spatial effect is difficult to illustrate clearly.

In our schematically drawn illustrations, the three main parts are represented symbolically by means of a circle, square and triangle which have been drawn at the end of the main lines. The principal branches are represented by solid-black symbols, and the supporting elements of the composition, such as individual flowers or small twigs, are represented by hollow triangles, squares or circles according to their relationship to the main part of the arrangement.

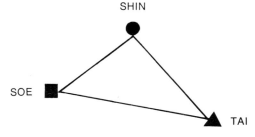

What do *Shin, Soe, Tai* signify?

SHIN = truth ●
This is the strongest, most important and often the longest element in the composition. In some ikebana schools, shin symbolizes heaven. The Ikenobo School sees in it a symbol of a man who has attained enlightenment.

SOE = support, help ■
According to its length and weight, soe is the second most important element of the arrangement. For most students of ikebana this line symbolizes man situated between heaven and earth.

TAI = body ▲
In many ikebana schools, tai symbolizes the earth. This is the smallest and shortest segment of the arrangement.

How long are the main lines?

The length of the main lines is in proportion to the size of the container and the kinds of plant used.
A rule of thumb for the beginner is:

$$\text{length of shin} = \left[\begin{array}{l}\text{diameter} \\ \text{of container}\end{array} + \begin{array}{l}\text{height of} \\ \text{container}\end{array}\right] \times 1.5 \text{ to } 3$$

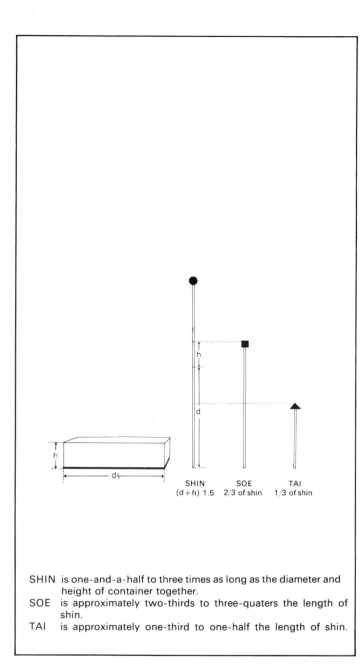

SHIN   SOE   TAI
(d + h) 1.5 2/3 of shin 1/3 of shin

SHIN is one-and-a-half to three times as long as the diameter and
         height of container together.
SOE   is approximately two-thirds to three-quaters the length of
         shin.
TAI   is approximately one-third to one-half the length of shin.

MORIBANA
UPRIGHT STYLE A
Moribana chokutai A

Plants   three oak branches, three chrysanthemums
Container   round, black ceramic bowl
              diameter 25 cm, height 4.5 cm

Both plants used here are resilient, hearty, robust and make a somewhat serious, ponderous impression. They grow slowly. Among some western peoples, the oak enjoys great respect as a symbol of freedom and power. The chrysanthemum is Japan's national flower. Therefore, a possible theme for this simple arrangement might be the symbolic co-operation between East and West.

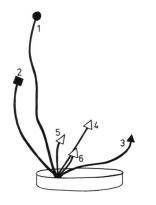

Sketch of composition

In this upright style, **shin** stands vertically in the kenzan, or else is slanted at a 30° angle (illustration IV, front elevation). For this style only straight branches and flowers are suitable. Cascading branches or those spreading sideways will be used for hanging compositions.

●   **Shin**   here slants at about a 10° angle leaning to the left front.

■   **Soe**   slants at about a 40° angle leaning to the left back.

▲   **Tai**   slants here at about a 75° angle pointing to the right front.

△△△   **Tai**-fillers **(Ashirai** or **Jushi)** nod amiably to the front.

Position of stems in flower holder (Plan)

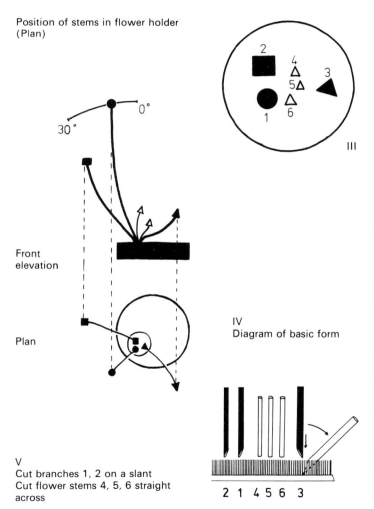

III

IV
Diagram of basic form

V
Cut branches 1, 2 on a slant
Cut flower stems 4, 5, 6 straight across

Front elevation

Plan

2 1 4 5 6 3

In Moribana never place the needlepoint holder in the centre of the container, but always to the left or right in the bowl. In this arrangement the kenzan is placed to the left front.

For **shin** use a sturdy, straight branch. It should be about 1.5 to 2 times as long as the sum of the diameter and height of the ceramic bowl (here 46–60 cm). Cut the branch on a slant (illustration V), place it vertically on the point marked in the flower holder (illustration III) and bend it slightly to the left (approximately 10°).

The second branch, **soe,** is about two-thirds the length of shin. It is also cut on a slant (illustration V). First place it vertically in the kenzan behind shin and then bend it about 40° to the back left.

The third branch is **tai.** It is approximately one-third the length of shin. Place it to the right of shin in the kenzan and bend approximately 75° to the front right.

The three **flowers** are cut to different lengths. The longest stem (4 in illustration II) should not be longer than one-third of shin. It is placed in the centre of the kenzan between the shin and tai branches. The other two flowers (5 and 6) are placed in front of it (as shown in illustration III). The flowers slant slightly to the front. They should not be too short, otherwise, they give the impression of having been cut off at the rim of the bowl.

The ends of the branches form an irregular triangle. Depth and spatial effect are achieved by placing the flowers one behind the other.

49

LESSON 2

Plants   two yellow sweet sultan *(Centaurea)*
            three dark blue irises
Container ceramic bowl in form of a ship with feet

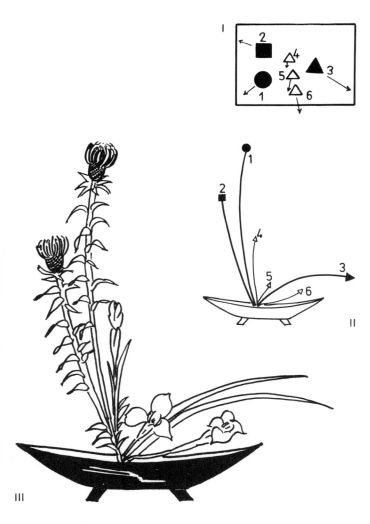

We are once again going to practise the important ikebana basic style seen in the last lesson. This time we are going to use only flowers.

Shin and soe are going to be represented by the centaureas, while tai is represented by the blossoms and leaves of the irises.

Cut all flowers straight across just as we did to the chrysanthemums in the first lesson.

Shin (1) slants slightly to the front left, soe (2) is placed behind shin and slants at 30° to the back left. Tai (3) slants at approximately 70° to the front right. The longest iris (4), approximately two-fifths to one-third the length of shin, is placed in the centre slanting slightly to the front.

The next iris (5) is about one-fifth the length of shin and slants to the front.

The third iris (6) slants to the front right and measures about one-third the length of the shin stem.

Variations

In place of centaureas for shin and soe, liatris, larkspur, eremurus, monk's-hood, lupin or loose-strife can be used.
With liatris use blue or yellow irises, three pink carnations, five marguerites or five red roses
With larkspur, monk's hood and lupin use pink roses, dark pink or yellow carnations, peonies, yellow daisies, yellow irises or yellow lilies
With loose-strife use dark blue campanulas, irises or cornflowers
With eremurus use tiger-lilies, dark blue irises, deep red or deep lilac dahlias.

50

Plants   sloe branches, tulips or daffodils
Container Japanese ceramic bowl with feet
             or round German ceramic bowl

The Ikebana student's work space is made ready for the next lesson as in the photograph. Take the branches and flowers out of the water pail. Have the ceramic bowl, some flower wire in different strengths, a two-piece flower holder, and the ikebana scissors ready for use. The flower bowl should already be filled with water so that we can cut the flowers under water. Always replace the scissors on the cloth to avoid making noise.

Plan of position in kenzan

Sketch of composition

Shin (sloe branch 1) slants to the front right at approximately 20°.

Soe (sloe branch 2) is about two-thirds the length of shin and slants to the back left at about a 45°–50° angle.

Tai (tulip 3) is placed in the centre of the kenzan, is approximately one-third the length of shin and slants towards the front. The tai-fillers (4 and 5) are tulips of different lengths which are placed in front of tai slanting slightly forward.

51

The student's arrangement is shown here in two different ceramic bowls. One can see that the slightly higher Japanese bowl is less well suited to these branches. The container appears too narrow. A feeling of springtime is not conveyed. The same composition in the shallower, wider, egg-coloured bowl gives a greater feeling of freshness.

Here we see the arrangement after it has been corrected by the teacher. The lines of the branches have been made visible by the teacher's cutting away some of the leaves and twigs according to the principle: less is more. Simplification is an important principle in every Japanese flower arrangement. Only then can the beauty of the lines and forms be enjoyed, too much fullness causes them to be lost. In this example, we see how important it is to move the kenzan from the centre.

Plants   cherry tree branches with buds
               three red tulips
               three yellow freesias *(Freesia refracta)*
Container half-moon shaped ceramic bowl with feet

Flower arrangements in winter are attractive as well. If there are no leafy branches available, use bare ones instead. For this composition it is best to choose flowers with leaves, such as tulips, or evergreen branches. A winter arrangement should also convey a feeling of life. It can express the expectation of spring.

The tulip originated in Turkey and is now to be found everywhere in the world. Numerous kinds and newly cultivated varieties of tulips are available in the most varied colours, shapes and sizes. The stems cannot be bent as they break easily.

Even in the vase, tulips grow sometimes as much as 1–2 cm per day and must therefore be cut back to size.

Lovely, large surface, tulip leaves can also be used without blossoms. Try once to make a Moribana arrangement using only tulips! (*Isshu-ike* — arrangements made of just one kind of plant.) Pay special attention to the leaves!

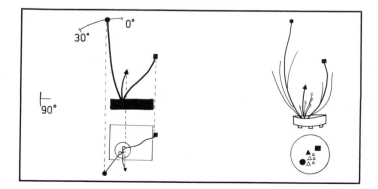

53

Plants   three gladiolas
Container   rectangular ceramic bowl

1 The first gladiola is shin.
2 The second flower to the right is soe.
3 A gladiola cut short and bent forward is tai.
4 Shin-ashirai is made up of leaves.
5 Soe as well is given filler lines of leaves.
6 Tai-ashirai leaves slant to the front.

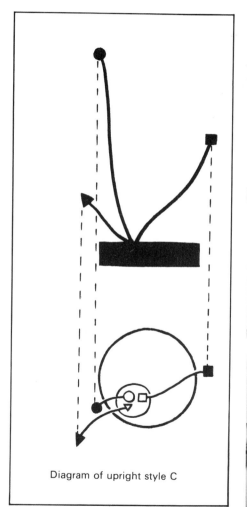

Diagram of upright style C

1 Method of cutting off the tip of a leaf.
2 Always cut leaves off with a piece of the stem.
3 Method of bending a gladiola leaf.
4 Method of bending a gladiola leaf.
5 Method of rolling a gladiola leaf.

	3
1	4
2	5

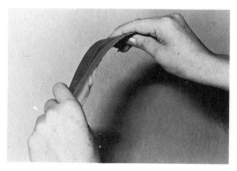

55

Plants   branches of a Korean honeysuckle *(Lonicera)*
              red spray carnations
Container   light brown rectangular ceramic bowl with feet

With these graceful curving lines we vary the upright Moribana style. We can enjoy the gentle, softly curving lines at all times of the year. The small-blossomed spray carnations harmonize with these lines. Moss-roses, freesias and anemones can also be used. At summer's end, the branches of the honeysuckle are decorated with glowing red berries. White daisies go well with these.

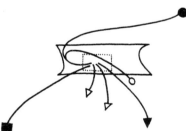

Plan

The following five illustrations show the step-by-step procedure for making this arrangement. The angle of inclination of the branches can be seen in this drawing. The plan demonstrates the direction of each individual line.

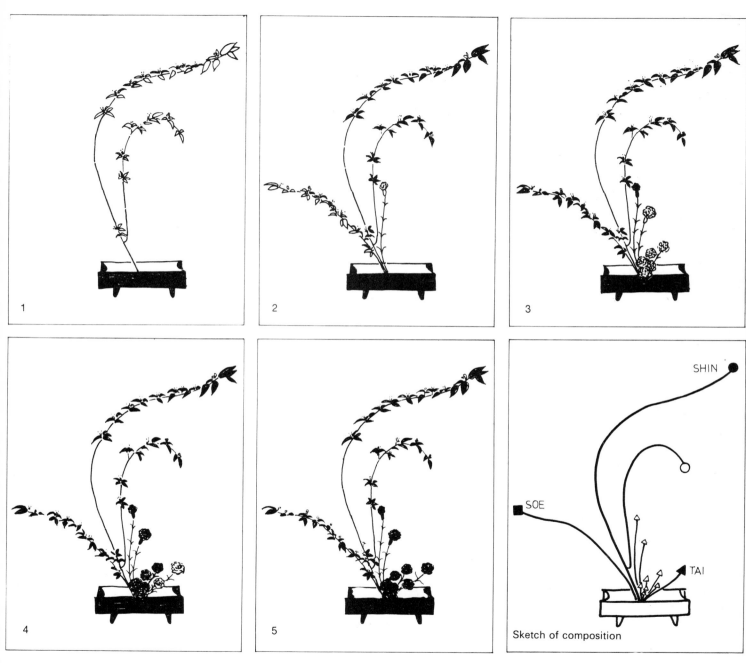

1

2

3

4

5

SHIN

SOE

TAI

Sketch of composition

57

Plants   two reeds with leaves *(Arundo phragmitis)*
        three dark blue irises
Container   black ceramic bowl in the form of a ship

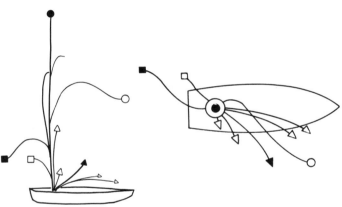

On a hot summer's day we like to be near a cool body of water. Blue iris flowers and the gentle movement of reeds can convey this feeling of coolness. The container as well reminds us of a lake.

This simple arrangement, with just a few lines and plants, transports us to a pond. It may remind us of the atmosphere and memories of a happy summer's day.

Reeds do not remain fresh very long in a floral arrangement. They have to be treated in a special way before beginning the composition. First, tap the cut end of the reed with the handle of your ikebana shears, then place the stalk in vinegar or diluted hydrochloric acid for about 5–10 minutes. After that, the plants should be placed in deep water for about two hours where they can recover. Only then can they be used in an arrangement.

Plants   bare branches covered with moss or lichen
             small chrysanthemums
Container half-moon shaped ceramic bowl with feet

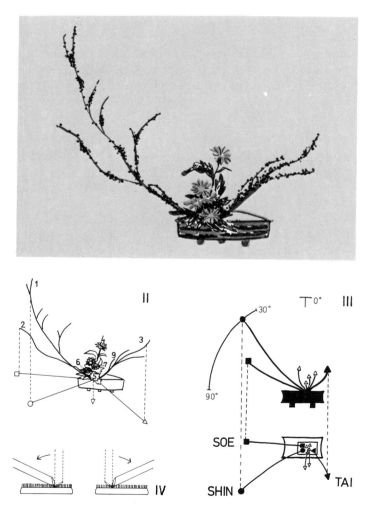

By using three branches and flowers, we create a November feeling. Winter is just around the corner. The slanting Moribana style is better suited to this season. In this style, the shin branch is slanted still further away from the vertical position. Its angle of inclination is between 30° and 90° (see illustration III).

Shin (1 in illustration II) is here twice as long as the sum of the diameter and height of the container. The branch is cut on a slant, then placed vertically into the kenzan (illustration IV) and finally bent to the front left (illustration III). Do the same with soe (2 in illustration II). Soe, two-thirds the length of shin, is placed behind shin in the kenzan and slants to the same side.

Tai is also a moss-covered branch (3 in illustration III), it slants at a 45° angle to the front right. A reverse of this composition would show the following: If shin and soe were slanted towards the right, tai would lean towards the front left. Just as the plan (illustration III) shows, the flowers have been placed in the centre of the kenzan. One chrysanthemum (4 in illustration II) is approximately two-fifths the length of shin and stands almost vertically. Another (5 in illustration II) slants rather far over the container's rim to the front. Between these two flowers the other three have been placed one behind the other in ascending order.

Small moss-covered branches (9) support tai when necessary. The slanting Moribana style is comparatively wide. For this reason the flowers should bring out the depth of the arrangement. No flowers appear from under shin and soe.

Plants   nine spiraea branches *(Spiraea vanhouttei)*
              with new leaves
              two dark blue irises
              three deep pink carnations
Container Japanese ceramic cup with light crystal glaze

Let's try an arrangement with many lines. Not only in ikebana, but in Japanese painting and caligraphy as well, lines play an important role. When all the branches of the composition project upwards from a single point, this symoblizes the power of early spring.

Other plant combinations

One can use other branches and flowers in accordance with the season and artistic inspiration. In place of spiraea, basket willow, sallow, privet, or almond branches can be used. Gentle buds and silvery catkins are favourite signs of spring.

Other flowers can be used too. Every new form and colour combination lends new charm and expression to ikebana compositions. If two different kinds of flowers are to be combined, contrasting colours or flowers which are differentiated in nuance of shade can be chosen. Don't combine flowers which are either very similar or strikingly different. One kind of flower should always serve as the focal point while the others play a supporting role. In this way, both kinds of flowers enhance each other. The following unfavourable combinations should be avoided in ikebana unless a special effect is strived for: gerberas and daisies, white lilies and amaryllis, roses and carnations, chrysanthemums and gerberas, dahlias, zinnias or daisies.

Be careful not to arrange the flowers indiscriminately but try to achieve a step-by-step ascending colour line receding towards the back.

Shin, soe and tai are formed of spiraea branches (illustration II). Shin (1) slants to the left and somewhat to the front. Soe (2) also slants to the left but somewhat to the back.

The linear movement of shin and soe must harmonize. Tai (3) is also made of branches and slants to the front right.

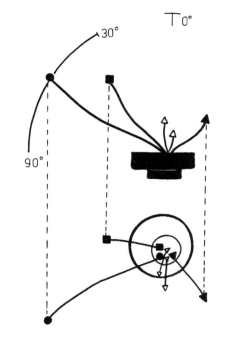

T 0°

30°

90°

II

Considering the size of our cup, the arrangement would certainly be too scanty if we were to use just one branch for each of the main parts of the ikebana. This would also contradict the natural growth of the spiraea. For this reason we are going to use some fillers (Ashirai) for each of the main lines. Branches 4, 5 and 6 (illustration III) serve as shin-ashirai. Two further branches (7, 8) serve as soe-ashirai, they are arranged slanting towards the back between shin and soe. Both irises including their leaves (9, 10) stand to the right of soe as another soe-ashirai. Small spiraea branches (11, 12) support tai and so do the three carnations (13, 14, 15). One should pay special attention to the lowest carnation (15) which should bend quite far over the rim of the container. Don't cut too short!

III

1	**Shin**	(spiraea)
2	**Soe**	(spiraea)
3	**Tai**	(spiraea)
4	**Shin-Ashirai**	(spiraea)
5	**Shin-Ashirai**	(spiraea)
6	**Shin-Ashirai**	(spiraea)
7	**Soe-Ashirai**	(spiraea)
8	**Soe-Ashirai**	(spiraea)
9	**Soe-Ashirai**	(iris with leaves)
10	**Soe-Ashirai**	(iris with leaves)
11	**Tai-Ashirai**	(spiraea)
12	**Tai-Ashirai**	(spiraea)
13	**Tai-Ashirai**	(carnation)
14	**Tai-Ashirai**	(carnation)
15	**Tai-Ashirai**	(carnation)

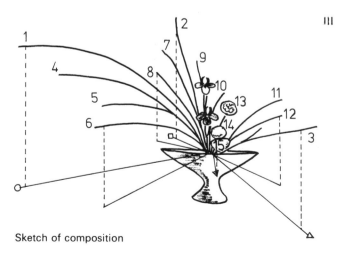

Sketch of composition

Plants   five cherry tree branches with buds
                     five salmon-coloured roses
                     five Japanese fern leaves, dried and bleached
Container ceramic bowl with feet, turquoise

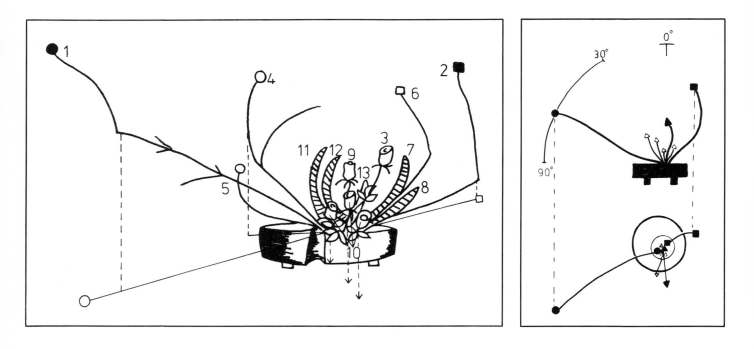

Only after you have closely observed branches, bare of leaves and blossoms in winter, for the first time, will you discover the beauty of the lines and various growth patterns. Bare cherry tree branches can also be arranged in a lively manner if one, as here, contrasts them with noble roses and the gentle white of ferns. The turquoise Ikebana bowl adds a note of freshness to the total effect.

White thorn or sloe branches lend an interesting touch too. Find variations.

This time we have placed the kenzan in the right hand side of the container. Just as in all compositions, it can also be placed to the left. The lines of the ikebana are then arranged in reverse order. This is done according to the branches you have, the place where the ikebana is to be

displayed, and the lighting available.

Shin (1) is composed of one long cherry tree branch which is first placed vertically into the kenzan (see lesson 8) and then slanted at a 70° angle to the left so that it leans slightly to the front left.

Soe (2) is about two-thirds the length of shin and slants to the back right. We have obtained an interesting line by cutting the main branch.

Tai (3) is composed of a rose blossom supported by fillers of roses (9, 10) and fern leaves (11, 12, 13).

Shin-ashirai (5, 4) is made of branches, soe-ashirai of one branch (6) and two fern fans (7, 8). Make sure that the roses slant well to the front towards the observer. They should not disappear behind the rim of the bowl.

Plants   branches of mountain-ash (rowan tree, *Sorbus aucuparia*)
             three roses
Container black, matt-finished ceramic cup

Mountain-ash branches bring joy at any time of the year. They are especially attractive in spring with their buds and young leaves. In the spring, mountain-ash branches are called *raidenboku* in Japan, then in the summer, *nanakamado* when they are covered with their peculiar feathered leaves. In some containers and with whatever flowers are used, the leaves of this branch have an overpowering effect. Therefore, we do not hesitate to cut off many leaves for only then is a filigree effect achieved.

Variations

In place of roses, we can combine blue irises with the mountain-ash, or we can use tiger-lilies or dahlias. In the autumn, when the branches bear glowing red berry clusters, chrysanthemums or asters are best suited.

Plants   three fern leaves
              three funkia *(Hosta)* leaves
              five roses
Container   ceramic bowl in form of a half circle with feet

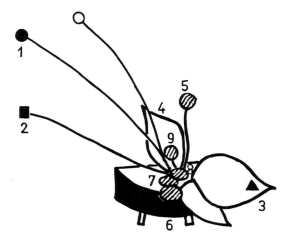

We tie together two fern leaves of different lengths with flower wire. These form shin which slants to the front left (1). For soe (2) another fern leaf is arranged behind shin.

Two funkia leaves form tai. They lean towards the front right. As background for the group of roses, we place a third leaf behind shin in the kenzan (4). One rose (5) is set in the centre reaching up to about half the height of the composition. A further blossom (6) is placed in front, while the others (7, 8, 9) are arranged in a row between them starting with the smallest in front.

Roses are delicate and should therefore always be cut under water. Further tips concerning the handling of flowers are to be found in the last section of this book (see page 179). Leaves with large surfaces are well suited to ikebana, but we only find them in Europe in the warmer southern areas. We can improvise by using house plants such as sansevieria, asphodel, rubber-tree, philodendron phoenix, dracaena or codiaeum.

Plants   Virginia creepers with tendrils *(Parthenocissus quinquefolia)* five pink roses

Container light blue ceramic cup made by combining a cylindrical vase and a small bowl. Bowl and vase can be used separately or combined (illustration I)

In the Moribana hanging style *(Moribana suitai)* the angle of inclination of the shin branch is between 90° and 180° (an imaginary line rising vertically from the kenzan signifies 0).

All hanging branches and tendrils are suitable for suitai. In our example we use a tendril of Virginia creeper to represent shin (1). If we were to arrange the shin branch exactly according to the scheme of the basic form, the reverse side of the vine leaves may be turned upwards. In this instance we can make the arrangement as a mirror image. The linear movement of the shin branch follows that of the soe-line (2) but just a little further to the front right. Its length is approximately two-thirds that of shin.

Tai (3) consists of a high upward reaching branch of Virginia creeper, slanting somewhat to the back left.

Just as in the preceding lessons, place one rose in the centre (4) and let another one face the front (5). The other three roses are arranged between (4) and (5).

A pair of vine leaves behind the blooms enhances the beautiful glow of the roses and makes them prominent.

Variations

Try using another container. Perhaps you have a tall chalice made of glass or metal.

Moribana suitai makes an especially good autumn arrangement when you use the fiery red of the vine leaves. Ivy, as well, offers new ways to vary expression and atmosphere.

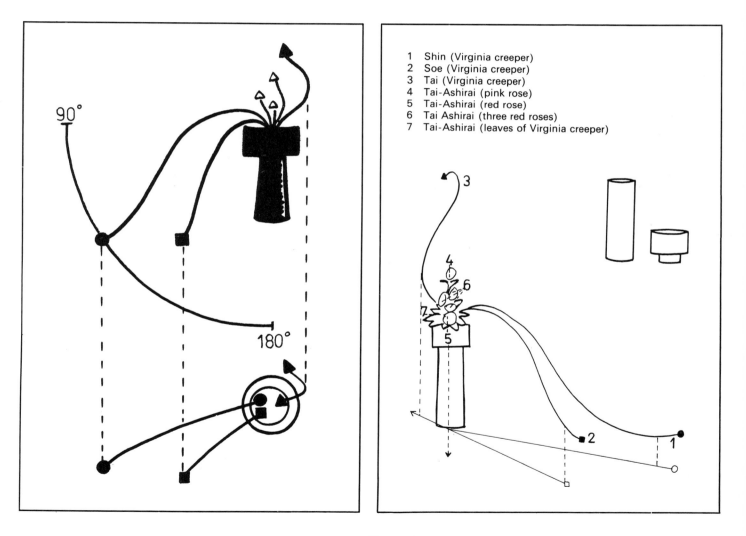

90°

180°

1 Shin (Virginia creeper)
2 Soe (Virginia creeper)
3 Tai (Virginia creeper)
4 Tai-Ashirai (pink rose)
5 Tai-Ashirai (red rose)
6 Tai Ashirai (three red roses)
7 Tai-Ashirai (leaves of Virginia creeper)

1

2

3

4

5

6

7

Plants   three evergreen honeysuckle branches *(Lonicera pileata)*
                five daffodils
                ten daffodil leaves
Container brown ceramic cup

When we compare this arrangement (illustration I) with the plan (II), we realize that it has been arranged as a mirror image of the one described. Every once in a while, we can arrange the opposite style and compare the effect. Should the room for which this ikebana has been planned open to the right with a wall on the left side, then the variation with shin towards the right should be chosen. The hanging style emphasizes the long curving line of the honeysuckle branch. The shin-line (1 in illustration IV), which points forward to the right, sets the tone for the entire arrangement: positive, cheerful, fresh and uncomplicated, springlike and spirited (illustration III).

Soe, the second branch, measuring two-thirds of the shin branch, also supports the valid 'truth' of this composition and curves in a similar fashion upwards to the right (2 in illustration IV).

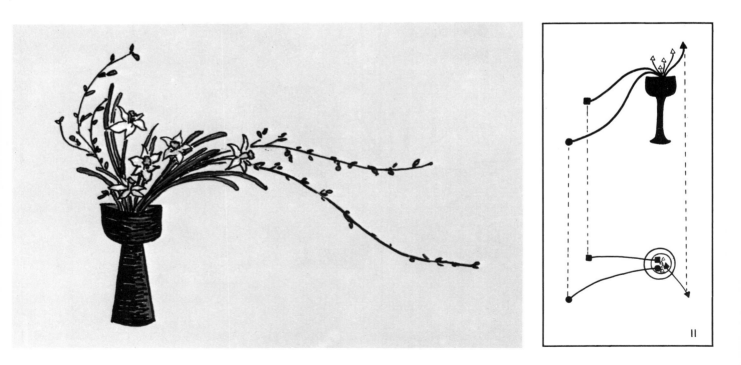

In order to balance the arrangement, tai (3) towers above the composition in a straight line with the tip following the main line. If tai were to hang, it would create a feeling of sadness.

Fresh daffodil leaves and pale yellow blossoms serve as ashirai underlining that which we have tried to express in the three lines of shin, soe and tai (4–11 in illustration IV).

Blossoms 10 and 11 stretch freshly towards the front and over the rim of the cup. This, however, cannot be clearly shown in the drawing. Several leaves face towards the back (12) and towards the front left (13), thereby creating spatial effect.

The daffodil leaves are of special importance. When buying these flowers, pay special attention to this. The gentle curve in the leaves needed for this composition is achieved by running them carefully through your fingers.

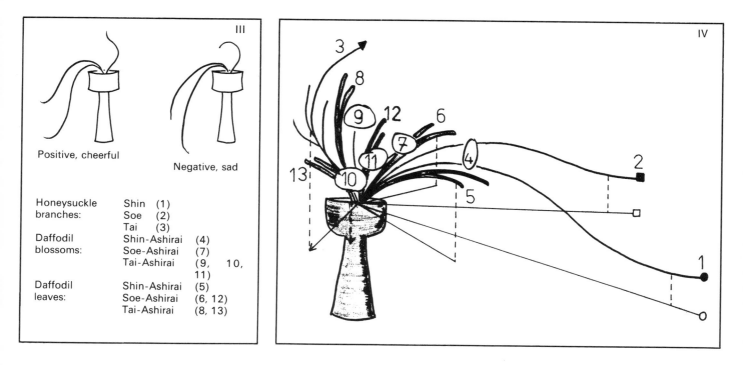

III	
Positive, cheerful	Negative, sad

Honeysuckle branches:	Shin	(1)		
	Soe	(2)		
	Tai	(3)		
Daffodil blossoms:	Shin-Ashirai	(4)		
	Soe-Ashirai	(7)		
	Tai-Ashirai	(9,	10,	
		11)		
Daffodil leaves:	Shin-Ashirai	(5)		
	Soe-Ashirai	(6, 12)		
	Tai-Ashirai	(8, 13)		

LESSON 15

Plants   branches of rose spiraea *(Spiraea bumalda)*
            three red gerbera
            fescue grasses *(Festuca rubra)*
Container blue ceramic bowl with feet

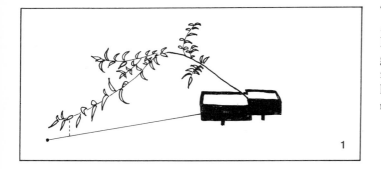

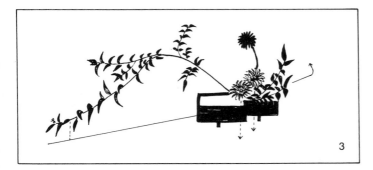

The kenzan is located in the right hand side of the container. A step-by-step arrangement is given in these illustrations. For shin a spiraea branch is used (1). Soe comprises one gerbera and several short branches which bend to the back right (2). The gerbera blossoms which represent tai should lean far forward (3). The composition ends on a harmonious note with the slightly bent fescue grass (4, 5).

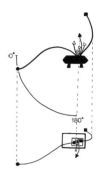

Variations can be obtained by using other plants, for
example forsythia, cotoneaster, honeysuckle or privet.

Plants	branches of weeping willow three red tulips
Container	dark blue, round ceramic bowl
Theme	spring winds

How simple materials can conjure up a whole world!

Plants
  Zebra grass *(Miscanthus sacchariflorus zebrinus)*, Chinese campanula *(Campanula platycodon* 'grandiflorum'), *Patrinia scabiosifolia*
Container
  Japanese bamboo basket
Style
  Moribana, upright style
Master
  Masahiro Ikeda (Koryû)

MORIBANA

The Charm of Impermanence

If in the highlands
Not only for these short days
In silver shimmer
Would bloom the old cherry trees
We would not deeply love them.
    (Yamabe no Akihito, 675)

Master
    Masahiro Ikeda (Koryû)

MORIBANA

Plants
   Magnolias, Hydrangea hortensia
Container
   Ashidaka-Suiban (ceramic bowl with three high feet)

Style
   Combination of horizontal and slanting style of Moribana
Master
   Masahiro Ikeda (Koryû)

MORIBANA

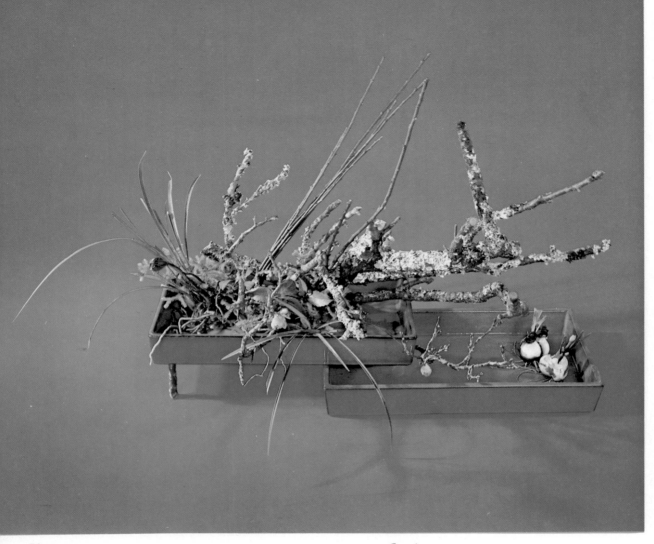

Plants
　Large plum branch with lichen, medium-sized plum branches,
　young plum branches, plum sprouts, Japanese orchids with
　roots, chloranthus glaber, daffodil bulbs, old Japanese cedar

Container
　Two partially overlapping, large, rectangular
　ceramic water pans
Style
　Moribana — landscape arrangement
Master
　Kumada Kôshû (Saga — Goryû)

MORIBANA

4

Plants
  Loquat *(Eriobotrya japonica) Chrysanthemum*
  segetum, aster
Container
  Ceramic vase composed of three attached cylinders

Style
  Upright parallel arrangement
Master
  Masahiro Ikeda (Koryû)

MORIBANA

5

Plants
  Aspidistra leaves,
  pomegranate
  (Punica granatum)
Container
  Igayaki ceramic bowl
Style
  Moribana free style
Master
  Sôfû Teshigahara
  (Sôgetsu School)

MORIBANA

6

Plants
    Small red and white
    chrysanthemums
Container
    Oblong raised bowl with base
    and thick glaze
Style
    Creative Moribana, upright
    style
Master
    Hôun Ohara (Ohara School)

MORIBANA

Plants
  Dried lotus fruits, withered wood,
  rose hips, small yellow
  chrysanthemums, dried lotus
  leaves
Container
  Large ceramic water tray with feet
Style
  Moribana — landscape
  arrangement
Master
  Hôun Ohara (Ohara-ryû)

MORIBANA

8

Plants
  Two *Dieffenbachia,* five red roses
Container
  Bluish green milk glass
Master
  Taiun Goshima (Ohara-School)

MORIBANA

Plants
  Wisteria with pods,
  chrysanthemums
Container
  Ceramic vase
Style
  Nageïre, slanting style
Master
  Kasumi Teshigahara (Sôgetsu)

NAGEÏRE

Plants
    Chinese lilac, small daffodils
Container
    A pair of Italian ceramic vases

Style
    Nageïre — combination
Master
    Sôfu Teshigahara (Sôgetsu)

NAGEÏRE

11

Plants
   Six clematis with tendrils
Container
   Small Japanese basket
   with delicate handle
Style
   Nageïre, slanting style
Master
   Masahiro Ikeda (Koryû)

NAGEÏRE

12

Plants
   Cosmos
Container
   Unusual, yellow glazed ceramic
   vase
Style
   Combination of upright and
   hanging Nageire styles
Master
   Masahiro Ikeda (Koryû)

NAGEÏRE

SIGN OF SPRING

NAGEÏRE

Plants
    Narcissus and leaves, vetches
Container
    Ceramic vase by Man-no-suke with three mouths
Style
    Nageïre, free variation
Master
    Fujiwara Yûchiku (Ikenobô School)

Plants
    Evening primrose
    (Oenothera), wild roses
Container
    Modern ceramic vase with feet
Style
    Nageire
Master
    Shûko Oda (Ohara School)

NAGEÏRE

Plants
  Juniper, bird-of-paradise
  (Strelitzia reginae) flower,
  alocasia
Container
  Ancient Japanese bellied vase
  (tsubo), wooden table (kadai)
Style
  Nageire
Master
  Toshi Yagi (Ohara School)

NAGEÏRE

Plants
    Sakura (Japanese double
    cherries), camellias
Container
    Ancient chinese tsubo vase on a
    tray made of cloud shaped root
    (*kadai kumogata*)
Style
    Nageire, combination of
    horizontal and slanting style
Master
    Hôun Ohara (Ohara School)

NAGEÏRE

Plants
Zebra grass
(Miscanthus 'zebrinus'), lily,
Stauntonia hexaphylla
(mube/Jap.)
Container
Unglazed, high,
ceramic vase
Master
Taiun Goshima
(Ohara School)

NAGEÏRE

18

EARLY SUMMER FEELING
SHÔKA NO KORKORO

Plants
    Purple bellflower, iris, honeysuckle
Containers
    Yellow, ship form, ceramic bowl with feet
Style
    Modern Shôka-Sanshu-ike

When one sees the high bellflower (which blooms in June) one thinks of the early summer.

We gladly use this upward stretching flower as Shin and place it in the middle.

The second bellflower follows as Shin Ashirai placed somewhat to the left in the kenzan behind Shin.

Three irises serve as Dô. We use honeysuckle to form Soe and Tai.

The straight lines of the bellflower and iris contrast with the fine curves of the branches. The yellow points in the dark purple iris blossoms are repeated in the glazed pattern of the container.

In place of bellflowers, gladiolas, foxgloves, larkspurs or monk's-hood can be used.

Master
    Shûsui-Pointner-Komoda (Ikenobô)

SHÔKA

Plants
  Pussy-willows, camellias
Container
  Large, flat ceramic water tray (Suiban)
Style
  Seika arrangement in the Saga Goryû style
Master
  Isseki Kusunoki (Saga School)

SHÔKA

20

HALF MOON

The Moon
When I look at the moon
I feel myself lonely
A thousand times.
But the autumn
Does not belong to me alone.
(Oeno Chisato, ninth century)

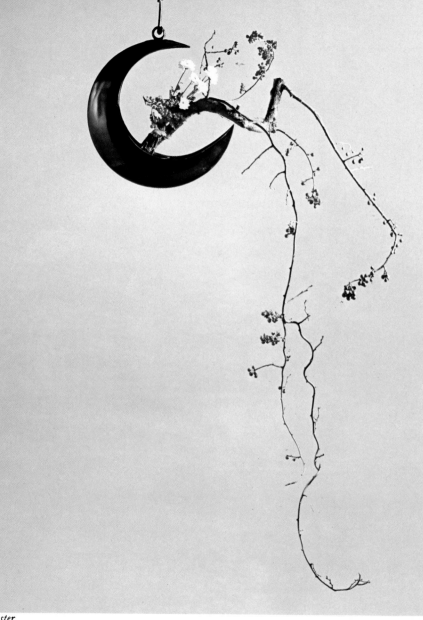

Master
Isseki Kusunoki (Saga School)

SHÔKA

21

Plants
  Aspidistra elatior, small chrysanthemums
Container
  A pair of wooden well buckets, a well rope serving as a tray
Style
  Seika
Master
  Isseki Kusunoki (Saga–Goryû)

SHÔKA

Plants
　Plum branches with shoots,
　roses, old moss-covered
　branches
Container
　Specially styled water container
　with feet
Style
　Seika
Master
　Isseki Kusunoki (Saga–Goryû)

SHÔKA

23

Spring has already gone,
The days hurry then towards summer,
For up on top of the cliff
The wind causes summer dresses to
flutter.
(Jitô Tennô, 645–702)

Style
   Seika
Master
   Shishû Kobayashi (Saga–
   Goryû)

SHÔKA

24

Plants
  Red gladiolas, bleached
  mitsumata
Container
  Ceramic cup
Style
  Shôka (Seika)
Master
  Riei Ikeda (Koryû)

SHÔKA

Plants
    African lilies *(Agapanthus)*, yellow marsh
    marigold *(Nuphar)*
Container
    Japanese ceramic tray
Style
    Shôka (Seika) Sô Style
Master
    Yûchiku Fujiwara (Ikenobô)

SHÔKA

26

NIJU-IKE
(IKEBANA IN DOUBLE BAMBOO VASE)

Plants
Gladiolas, New Zealand flax, Japanese campanula
Container
Bamboo vase with two openings (Nijû)
Style
Shôka (Seika) Sô Style
Master
Yûchiku Fujiwara (Ikenobô)

SHÔKA

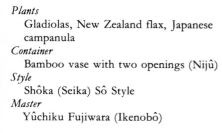

27

Plants
  Allium giganteum, Allium porrum, New Zealand flax, St.
  John's wort, peony, funkia leaves
Container
  Ceramic cup

Style
  Modern Rikka, Nokijin-style
Master
  Yûchiku Fujiwara (Ikenobô School)

RIKKA

28

Frog's Jump
What an ancient pond!
Splash of a frog's sudden jump.
Water's melody.
(Matsuo Bashô, greatest
Haiku poet, 1643–1694)

Plants
    Lotus buds, lotus leaves,
    hosta leaves, zebra grass
    (Miscanthus zebrinas),
    mountain lily, liatris
Container
    Ceramic vase with red glaze
Style
    Modern Rikka
Master
    Senei Ikenobô
    (Ikenobô School)

RIKKA

Plants
Pine, white plum blossoms, weeping willow, daffodils, bamboo
reed leaves (sasa)
Container
Three storey cylinder vase, ceramic

Style
Modern Rikka, Noki-jin style
Master
Yûchiku Fujiwara (Ikenobô)

RIKKA

30

Plants
    Turks cap lilies *(Lilium martagon)*,
    lily leaves, *Iris germanica,* gerbera,
    plum branches, peony leaves
Container
    Ceramic bowl in ship form with
    foot
Style
    Modern Nokijin-Rikka
Master
    Shûsui Pointner-Komoda
    (Ikenobô)

RIKKA

31

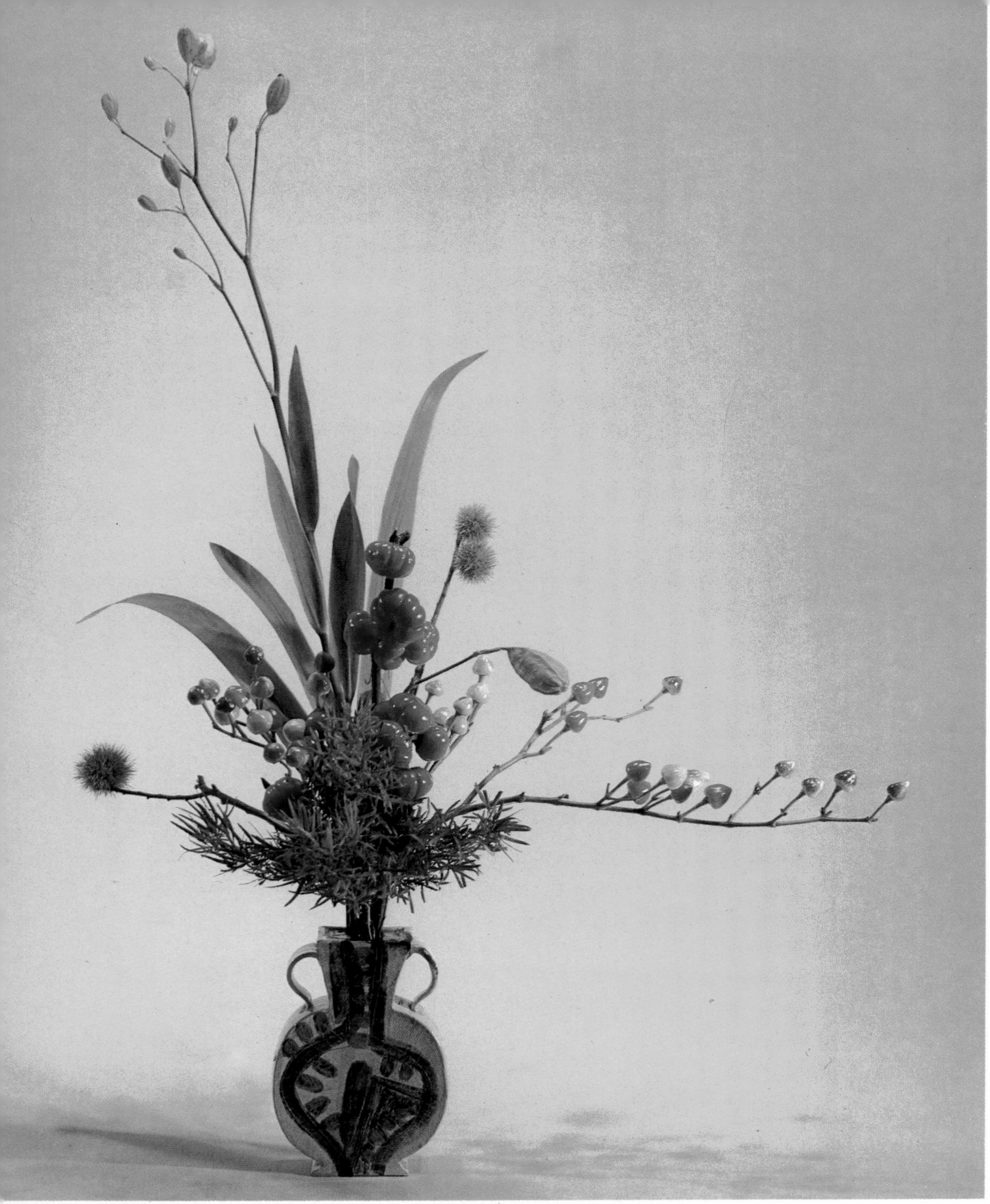

RICH HARVEST

Plants
Lily capsule, peppers, sweet chestnuts, decorative asparagus, leaves of *Iris japonica,* decorative peppers
Container
Ceramic vase
Master
Yûchiku Fujiwara (Ikenobô)

RIKKA

Questions for review:
In which style is this
ikebana arranged?
What is the meaning of
Moribana?
Indicate the main lines of
this composition.
After having answered the
questions please look back
at lessons 1 and 5.

LESSON 18   MORIBANA   LESSON 19   MORIBANA
                             VARIATION

Plants   willow-catkin branches   *Plants*   five reed maces (commonly called bulrushes)
            tulips with leaves   five garden carnations, dark red
                                                          one red gerbera blossom
                                                          small spiraea branches, autumn coloured
                                                          juniper branches
                                               Container black cast-iron bowl on three legs

Exercise: Exercises:
Try to draw a bird's eye view of this sketch in which can be   1. Indicate the main lines and fillers of this composition!
seen the direction of the various lines of the composition.   2. What is the style of this Moribana arrangement?

Plants   cherry laurel branches *(Prunus laurocerasus)*
                dahlias *(Dahlia cultorum)*
                Michaelmas daisies *(Aster novi-belgii)*
Container   large, light green Japanese ceramic
                water basin (suiban)

Futakabu-ike, the two-group Moribana demands a great deal of know-how and sensibility on the part of the arranger because a harmonious composition of both groups is necessary. Two-group arrangements were known far back in the history of ikebana, for example as two-group Rikka or Shôka.

Arrange both flower holders in the bowl as shown here in the diagram with the right hand kenzan towards the front, and the left hand one somewhat to the back.

For shin we use a cherry laurel placing it in the rear kenzan, and bending it slightly to the left front. Behind this, soe follows. Tai, slanting to the front right, is placed in the second, front flower holder.

A longer dahlia serving as soe-ashirai, and a smaller one as tai-ashirai are arranged together with a small daisy in the rear flower holder. In the front kenzan a dahlia has been added to the tai-line and a daisy serves as further filler material. The lines of these small flowers should integrate harmoniously.

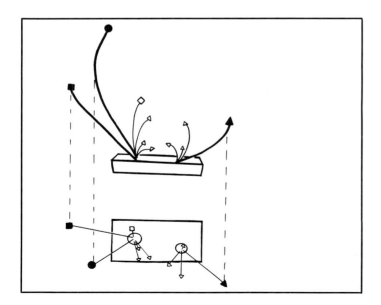

LESSON 21

Plants   forsythia branches, three tulips
Container   Suiban, large flat water basin with two kenzans

The exercise here was to express the theme 'pair' with the simplest floral material possible. To the left is the okabu or masculine part, to the right, mekabu, the feminine part. When the eye follows the linear movement it travels in a circle. The groups in this composition are placed at different distances from the observer's eye. The plan shows the movement of the lines towards the back and front.

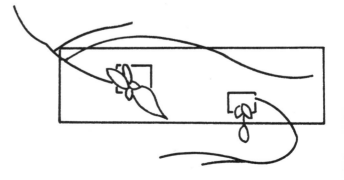

76

Plants   red and yellow chrysanthemums
                small yellow and white chrysanthemums
Container   Suiban, light green ceramic basin

This time, the left hand kenzan is placed towards the front. A red blossom, serving as shin (1) is placed in the kenzan, then slanted slightly towards the front left. Soe (2), on the other hand, a light blossom, turns towards the front left. Tai (3), comprising several small buds, is placed in the second rear kenzan and leans towards the front right. Then, the necessary ashirai fillers are added to both groups. The small blossoms in the background cause the right group to appear further away adding greater depth to the composition (overleaf).

Plants   green maple branches, pink gladiolas
Container oval flower bowl, pink glaze

This style of flower arrangement which has only been in practice for about thirty years, was taken from the repertoire of European and American flower decorations and adjusted to the needs of Moribana by several modern ikebana schools.

The very low 'placement' — here let's use this word for the first time — must have an appealing allure from all four sides. The observer does not have to place himself in a particular position as is the case in other ikebana styles, since the Shimentai style has no 'face'. Moribana, Nageïre, Shôka and Rikka, on the other hand, make a harmonious and balanced impression only from the front.

Japanese table arrangements of this kind are not as full and rich as the European. They are subordinate to the rest of the table decor, are assymetrical and comprise three main lines which form an irregular triangle.

Make sure that the water is clean and that no withered plant sections are visible. Flowers with very strong fragrances and heavy pollen are to be avoided and no element should tower over the other.

Both illustrations show the same composition, from the front (I) and from the back (II).

I

II

NAGEÏRE

What does Nageïre mean?

Nageïre is usually translated as 'throw-in arrangement'. Earlier, in Japan, people spoke of Nageïre-bana, 'thrown in flowers'. As we have already shown in the first section of this book, this relaxed, natural and less formal style of ikebana developed as a counterbalance to Rikka. Due to the influence of the tea ceremony, simple, elegant Chabana arrangements developed which can be regarded as forerunners of our modern Nageïre.

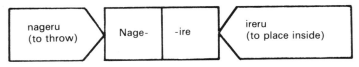

nageru (to throw) → Nage- -ire → ireru (to place inside)

Nageïre distinguishes itself from vase arrangements of the European kind largely by its asymmetry and lightness. This is obtained by using a very simple flower holder, the hana-kubari, made of a piece of branch, in order to hold the flowers and branches in place. This is quite different from the European manner of holding flowers in place by filling the vase opening full of flowers and branches.

Examples of Nageïre containers

Almost all kinds of vases are suitable for this ikebana style. They can be tall or short, cylindrical or square, simple or bizarre, with or without decoration, patterned or self-coloured, slender or bellied. There are no rules concerning the type of vase used except that it should conform to the needs of the flowers and the environment for which the Nageïre-arrangement has been planned. Just as in the case of the Moribana container, we advise choosing for a start a simple, sleek, timeless vase. It can be made of porcelain, clay, glass, wood or metal. Vases with very dark or quite light surfaces are more versatile than those with elaborate designs.

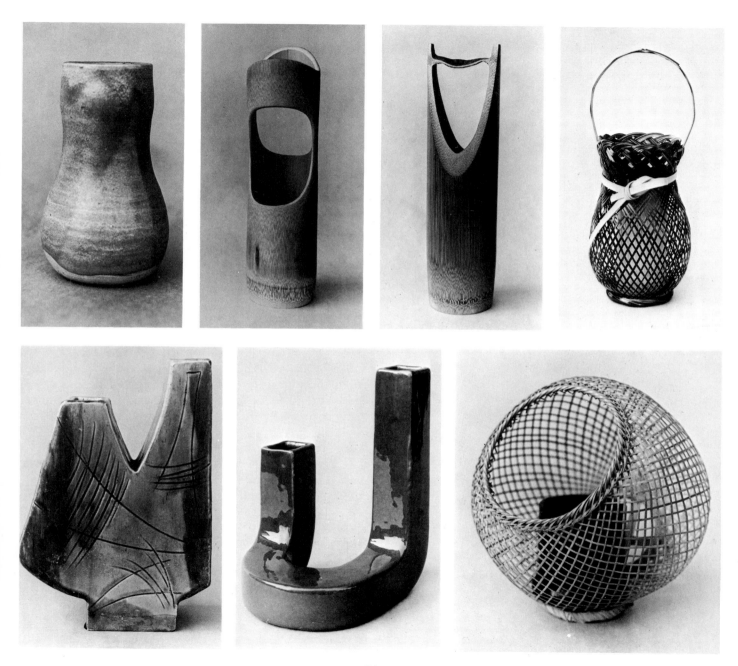

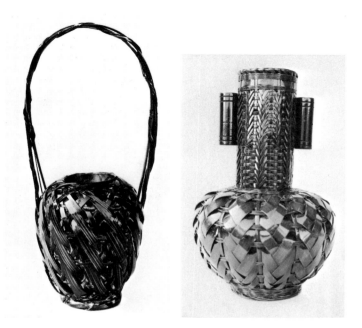

The illustrations demonstrate the most usual methods:

1. Here, the main branch has been split at the bottom and then bound by means of a piece of bast or flower wire to a piece of branch standing vertically in the vase. Without the help of the vertical *kubari* (flower holder, wooden stalk) the branch would turn downwards hanging in a sad manner.

2. In this example, the supporting stalk is locked into position vertically in the vase. This procedure is especially good for square, rimmed vases.

3. If, as is shown here, the wooden kubari is fastened to the branch, an elastic support results which can be clamped into the vase as shown in the illustration. The bottom end of the branch braces itself against the side of the cylindrical container.

4. The branch is bound to a kubari which has been firmly fitted into the vase. The branch and kubari should now fit snugly inside the container, touching the walls at three points.

5. According to the materials used and the style of the arrangement, various means of joining the pieces can be employed. Three of them are shown here. The method of fixing them in the vase is the same as in 4.

6. Be particularly careful when dealing with valuable porcelain vases or glass containers. In order to ensure that these do not become scratched or broken, wind a piece of cotton or other soft material around the ends of the kubari.

7. The most elegant way of fastening the kubari has been taken over from Shôka. However, this method is not suitable to all kinds of vases. The kubari always slips on slanting sides. If a forked stalk is not available, a branch from the arrangement can be split and used in the same way.

8. The easiest way of all is to use a heavy, wide and flexible lead strip.

How branches and flowers are held in the vase

The technique of holding flowers in a particular position in a vase, *Hana-dome,* has continued to improve in Japan. It is a question of lending a feeling of naturalness to floral arrangements. The flowers should not be bunched into the mouth of the vase and held in place in this way. On the contrary, they should appear to grow naturally out of the vase. If, at the same time, it can be arranged that as little of the stem as possible is submerged in water, less fouling will take place and the flowers will remain fresher longer. They can continue to absorb water as they are not compressed in the vase.

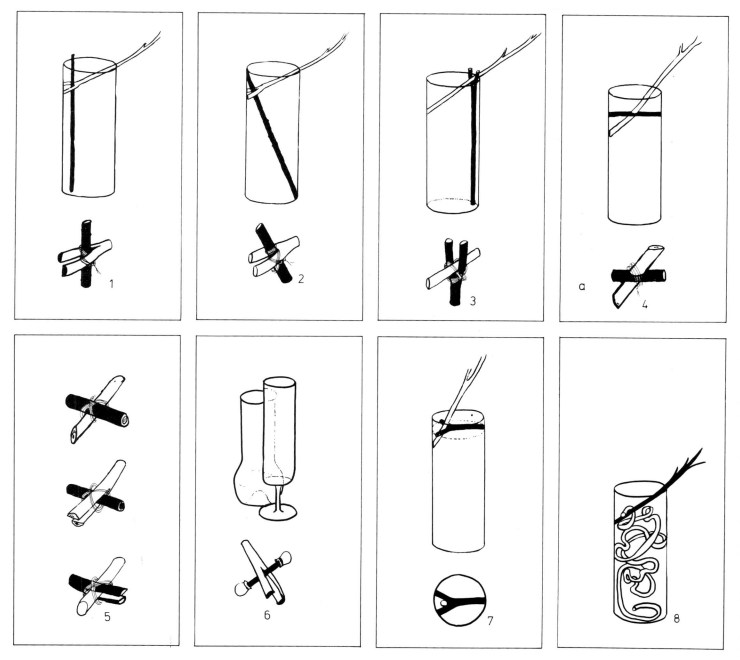

A suitable kubari for every Nageïre

The sketches on the right show 12 different hana-kubari variations. These are plan views representing cylindrical vases divided by kubari. The small circles represent the stalks of the flowers and branches. If the Nageïre is to be especially elegant the necessary plants should only be placed in one section. Naturally, this is often not possible due to the shape of the branches, and several of the sections at the mouth of the vase have then to be used. Heavy branches and large leaves have to be fastened to the kubari as we have seen on the previous page.

For some compositions a single kubari stick bound to the shin branch is enough to offer good support for further elements in the design. Whether the kubari is clamped into the vase from front to back (1), or from side to side (2), depends on the desired style, the plants and also the kind of vase being used. In most cases the main branches will lean either on the left or right rim of the vase (1, 3, 6, 9, 11). Sometimes, however, one wants to have the flowers rise up from the middle of the vase (5, 7, 8, 10, 12) or from the side of the arrangement away from the observer (4). Should no forked branch be available (4, 5), a stronger piece of wood can be forked and used to the same end.

How to bend branches

In order to obtain the desired degree of slanting and bending, plants that grow straight have to be bent, and naturally bent branches have to be straightened. This is especially necessary when various branches of the same tree or bush have to be combined harmoniously in one arrangement.

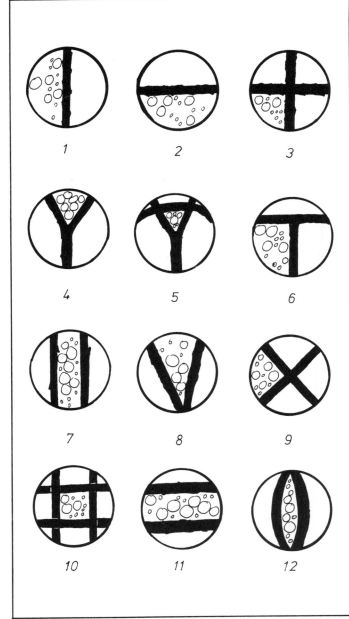

The methods used to bend a branch are dependent upon its kind and thickness. Some branches can hardly be bent at all (apple trees, pear trees, spiraea and maple). Others, however, can be bent very easily (all kinds of willows, juniper, pine trees and Japanese quince).

Methods

1. Hold the branch firmly in one hand as illustrated on page 116, pressing or twisting the branch somewhat together. A small crack is often not damaging (illustration 1, page 116).
2. Slight cuts can be made on the outside of the curve of some branches in order to lessen the strain on the bark at that point. Otherwise, the branch quickly returns to its original position (illustration 2, page 116).
3. When dealing with thicker branches, a wedge of the same wood is driven into the exterior curve. For this purpose, notches are made beforehand with shears or a small saw (illustration 3, page 116). Passionate ikebana enthusiasts plan ahead by binding branches in spring with bast or flower wire in the direction they want them to grow so that when they cut them in the autumn they have grown into the required shape.

Nageïre, parts and proportions

Just as in Moribana, Nageïre arrangements comprise three main elements: shin, soe and tai. These three main lines or masses are aided by filler elements (ashirai or jushi) just as in Moribana, and the ends or focal points form an irregular triangle whose surface stands neither vertically nor horizontally in the room.

It is the same in Nageïre as in Moribana — the length of the main branch depends upon the size of the vase. Here as well, the following rule of thumb is valid:

$$\text{length of shin branch} = \left[\text{height of container} + \begin{array}{c} \text{diameter} \\ \text{or width of} \\ \text{container} \end{array} \right] \times 1.5 \text{ to } 3$$

This means that the visible part of the shin branch is approximately one and a half to three times as long as the height and diameter of the container added together. When cutting to size, it must be taken into account that the branch is often placed deep into the vase depending on the way it is secured (hana-kubari). Therefore, to the above calculation is to be added the length of the non-visible part of the stem in the vase.

Soe and tai, just as in Moribana, depend upon the length of the shin branch. Soe measures approximately two-thirds to three-quarters the length of shin, and tai measures approximately a third to a half of it.

This rule of thumb can be of help to the beginner at the start. Advanced students will have developed their own feeling for proportions and will be guided as well by the size of the leaves, the various colours of the plants used, or their particular growth pattern.

Length of main lines in Nageïre

85

Plants   mountain-ash branches
             chrysanthemums
Container   high, round porcelain vase

Cut off a piece of mountain-ash branch corresponding to the diameter of the vase to act as kubari. Now fit the piece of wood into the vase underneath the upper rim. When cutting, do not take off too much at one time — one should work millimetre by millimetre. The kubari should fit snugly on its own in the vase.

Now take the kubari out again and bind, with bast or flower wire, the shin branch which has been cut down to the proper size. The resulting cross can now be fixed into place in the vase.

Whether you have decided to place the shin branch in such a way that it reaches to the bottom of the vase or leans on the upper part depends upon the kind of branch used and its natural curvature, and also on the shape of the vase. It is important that the shin branch stands upright and firmly fixed in place in the vase. It should not slant any further than 30° from the upright position and should slant slightly towards the front left.

In the illustration of the basic form, soe slants at approximately 45° to the left back. As you can see by this example, however, one never has to keep slavishly to one plan. In the present arrangement it seemed more suitable and prettier to have the soe branch slant to the front left. If it were arranged in accordance with the plan, soe would slant towards the back left revealing in the front the somewhat bare, straight lower section of the shin branch which might not be very appealing. But, as you will certainly not find the same branch, it is up to you to decide in what way you want to deviate from the present plan. Concerning this question, differences of opinion exist among the various ikebana schools. The Ikenobô School likes to have soe pointing to the back. As a supporting element of shin, soe should not push into the foreground, but, rather, fulfil its function by supporting the leading branch. In the basic form of the Sogetsu School, soe turns to the front. It can, when necessary, be fastened to the kubari by means of a piece of flower wire or bast, if it is not possible to clamp it into position so that it remains in place without help.

For tai we use the longest chrysanthemum. It slants at approximately 60° turning towards the front right.

Two more blossoms of the same colour serve as fillers (ashirai or jushi) for tai. The lowest of them projects furthest out towards the observer. If small blossoms are used, then four of them are necessary as ashirai to tai, making a total of five flowers.

Especially important in the upright style is the slender elegance of the arrangement. The rim of the vase should not be completely covered by plants in such a composition.

LESSON 25

Plants   delicate pink lilies
                 five sweet Williams
Container   cylindrical ceramic vase with pink glaze

As a kubari, clamp a wooden fork into the vase, opening to the right.

Now place the long lily vertically into this *hana-dome* (flower holder). This best matches the nature of this noble flower.

The five sweet Williams, all cut to different lengths, lean to the front left. This time, the length of the soe group does not conform to the rule of thumb given before. In this way, the upward stretching lily is placed to its best advantage. In this arrangement, soe really serves to underscore the linear movement of shin. Tai is also kept very short here. A lily bud and an open blossom lean forward over the rim of the vase.

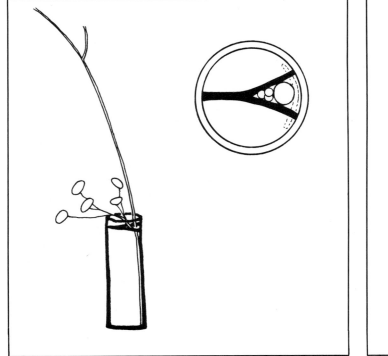

Always remember that ikebana is more than just blindly following rules! Ikebana demands a continual coming to grips with nature and plants. Within the traditional rules, ikebana leaves enough room for personal creativity.

Sketch of composition
1 Shin (long lily)
2 Soe (grass-of-parnassus)
3 Tai (buds and blossoms of the lily)

Plants   pussy willow *(Salix gracilistyla)*
                five pink tulips
Container   high, hand-turned vase

First look for a forked twig whose length equals the height of the vase, then fasten the shin branch to it with wire or bast so that both pieces together form an elastic Y. If you press them somewhat together, place them in a vase and then let go. They remain in place by force of elasticity (illustration II). Shin (1 in illustration III) rises straight upwards and slants somewhat to the front left.

At the point of junction of the shin branch and the vertical kubari, take some flower wire or bast and use this to bind the soe branch to the shin stem, so that the soe branch should turn somewhat to the back right. It is also advantageous if a little bit of wire is left over so as to hold the following elements in place. Make sure that the shin branch is tightly joined to the vase and difficult to displace, in this way it will be easier to fasten the other elements in the composition.

Five tulips form tai. The two upper blossoms stand almost vertically above the mouth of the container, while the three lower ones bend towards the front from the middle. Do not let the blossoms hang. You should pay special attention to the tulip leaves.

Give your arrangement a graceful, joyous, spring feeling! All kinds of willow branches are easily bent in almost every direction — with the right technique. Observe the instructions for bending branches which we gave before.

Try a variation of this composition by using other easily bent branches, like dogwood *(Cornus),* cherry branches *(Prunus)* or Japanese quince branches.

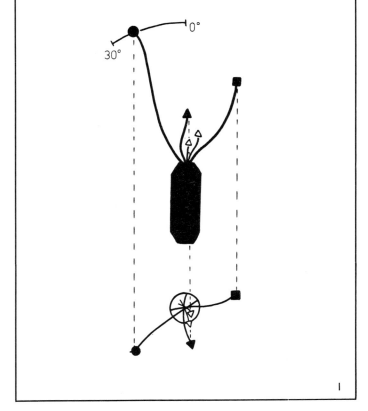

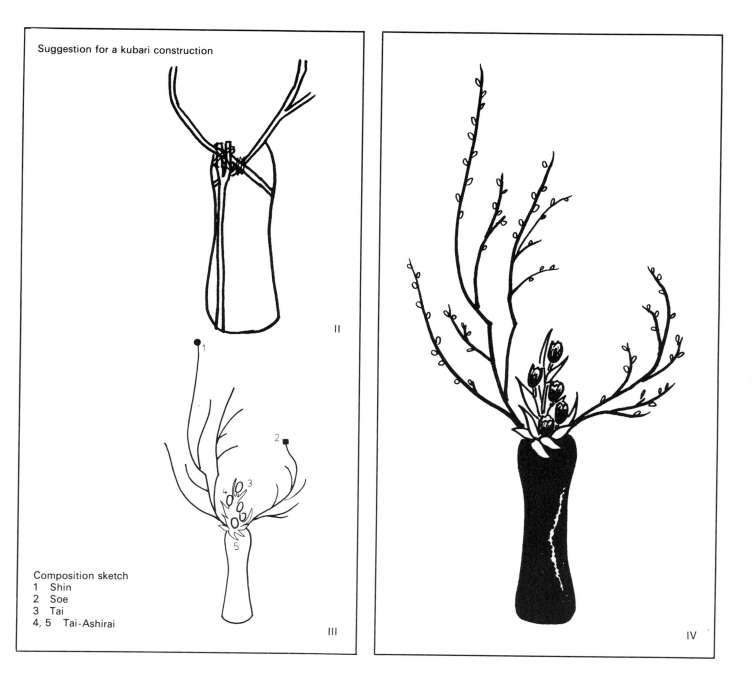

Suggestion for a kubari construction

II

Composition sketch
1 Shin
2 Soe
3 Tai
4, 5 Tai-Ashirai

III

IV

91

Plants   magnolia branches with dark violet buds
             two yellow roses
Container simple ceramic vase with dark blue glaze

Front
elevation

Plan

A piece of willow or dogwood branch serves us as the kubari (flower holder). We cut the branch to a length of about 1 cm longer than the height of the vase. The best diameter would be about 1.5 cm.

We cut into the top of the kubari stick, then clamp the shin branch into this slit. Using flower wire — here we use a stronger variety — a firm hold is established which, nevertheless, is elastic and remains clamped in the vase without help (1).

Soe is fastened to the kubari from the other side. It may hold better if we make a small notch in the wood with the shears at the joining point. The soe branch (2) slants to the right and a bit to the back, tai (3) slants to the front left.

We place both roses in the centre of the arrangement, making the stem of the closed blossom longer. The more open blossom is arranged to reach towards the observer.

We have to handle the magnolia branches with special care as the buds break off very easily.

The striking blossoms of the magnolia add a very strong accent so that they are often used in an Isshu-ike arrangement (a composition using only one kind of flower). One can use flowers in contrasting colours such as roses or peonies together with these large beautiful blooms.

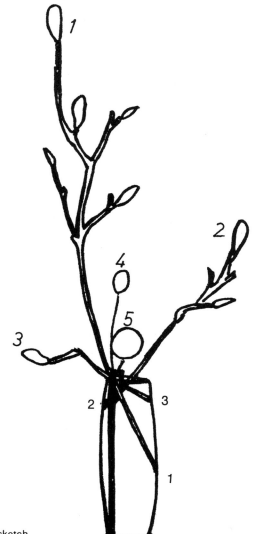

1

2

4

5

3

2　　　3

1

Composition sketch
with kubari drawn in

Plants   chestnut branches
               lilies *(Lilium auratum)*
Container   light green ceramic vase

The shin stem, here slanting to the side at an angle of about 50° and directed towards the front left, is fastened according to one of the methods described.

Behind it the soe branch is fixed. It executes an elegant curve to the back left. The photograph gives the impression that soe is almost as long as shin, and this true, but shin is heavier because it bears more thorny chestnuts and holds them out towards the observer.

Tai is formed by a lily bud turning towards the front right. Only then do the three main elements form a harmonious unit when the open lily blossom is added.

Possible variations are offered by the branches of apple tree, the Japanese quince, which can be found in many gardens, or the branches of the horse chestnut if a larger floor vase is used.

95

Plants	wild plum branches
	'Captain Fryat' tulips, red *(Tulipa retroflexa hybrida)*
	purple freesias
Container	black cylindrical ceramic vase

All three main lines are formed by plum branches: shin (1), soe (2) and tai (3). A long wooden stalk or a cross-piece can serve as hana-kubari as shown in the section dealing with nageire-technïque.

One of the tulips (4) bends slightly to the back right, the other two (5, 6) are arranged in the front centre. The freesias (7, 8) are arranged from centre to front. Special attention should again be paid to the tulip leaves. In place of plum branches, the branches of cherry, beech, whitethorn, or hazel trees can be used.

In the summer, many leaves have to be cut off the branches. This accentuates the line and also keeps the branches fresh longer because fewer leaves evaporate less water.

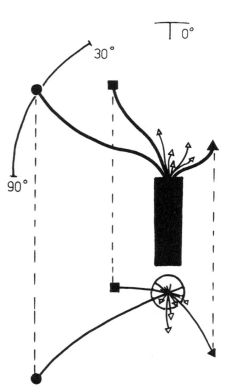

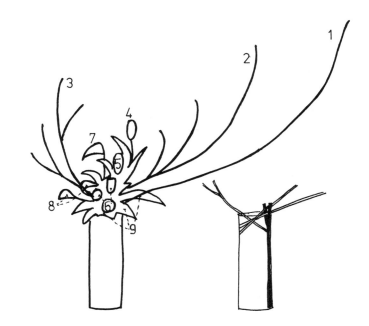

96

97

Plants   branches of red plum
                small yellow chrysanthemums
Container grey ceramic vase with dark brown glaze spots

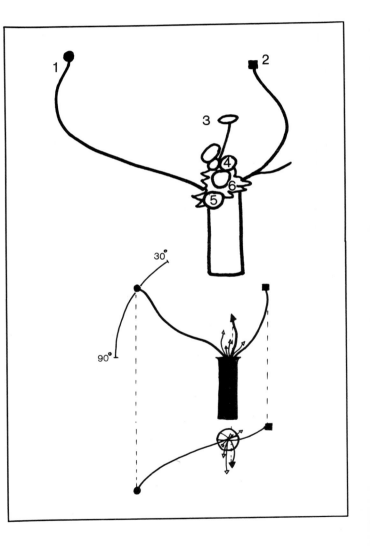

First decide what kind of hana-dome (flower holder) to use **after** you have held the branches alongside the vase. We have already made many kubari suggestions. You will, however, always have to invent new ones when arranging flowers simply because each branch is different in structure and weight. A good criterion for the proper fixing of the Nageïre pieces remains the fact that the shin branch should be fixed as snugly as possible into the vase so as to offer the other pieces enough support. It should stay in the desired direction and maintain its angle of inclination even when the vase is moved.

Our shin branch (1) is slanted at an angle of more than 60° and curves far out to the front left.

Soe (2) is fastened to shin with leftover flower wire so that it serves as a counterweight to shin on the right hand side turning somewhat to the back.

The tai group comprises chrysanthemum blossoms and leaves. The upper blossoms (3, 4) are all bending only slightly to the front, while the lower blossoms reach far out over the rim of the vase towards the observer.

The tray (kadai) made of a piece of wood is part of the arrangement and harmonizes with the colour of the red plum leaves. This kind of kadai which can be lacquered or left natural, made of bamboo, wood, or which might even be a small flat table, protects your valuable furniture from undesirable water spots.

99

Plants   spiraea branches
           bush carnations
Container ceramic vase with dark matt glaze

First fix the shin branch to a wooden fork (kubari) and then place it in the vase (1). Soe (2) and tai (3) lean between the kubari and vase rim since the mouth of this vase is quite narrow. The carnations are arranged in the centre and towards the front. According to their size, three, five, seven or nine blossoms are used.

The slanting style is best suited to tall vases. Expression can be varied by using other branches, almost any kind is suitable. The following are especially good for this composition; the branches of ash, whitethorn, sloe or dogwood.

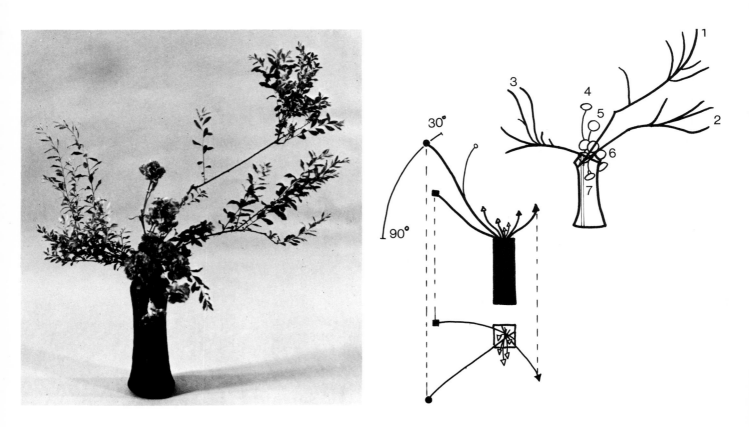

Plants   dogwood branches *(Cornus)*
            day-lily leaves
            daffodils
Container Japanese basket vase with porcelain inlay

It is important to have all plants, materials, containers and tools ready. Water is poured into the vase and a small cutting bowl before starting. Only when everything has been prepared, should you begin working on the composition. The natural peculiarities of the plants demand concentration. Flowers and plants are once again cut under water. The finished composition usually reflects something of its creator's mood.

Plants three spurge branches *(Euphorbia)*
two white lilies
Container square, black ceramic vase

Here, in this square vase, we clamp the kubari stick diagonally into the mouth of the container, as shown. Of course, we could also employ the vertical kubari depending upon the weight of the branch. Valuable, easily broken vases often do not allow for a horizontal kubari being forced in.

Just as with all other delicate plants, tie the spurge branches together with very fine flower wire or bast so that the vessels of the plant are not squeezed. Our arrangement is once again put together as a mirrored reflection of the basic pattern because the branches make it necessary.

Shin (1) and soe (2) curve very far to the front right

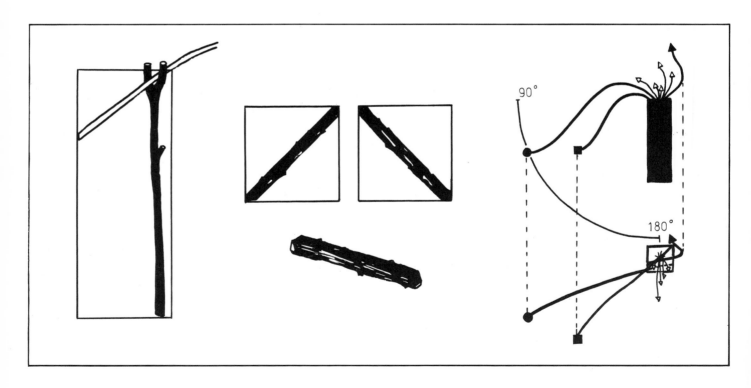

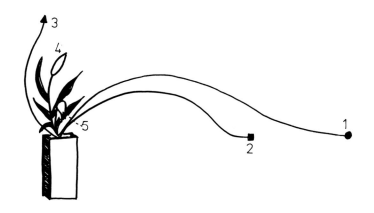

slanting in this Suitai style at an angle of between 90° and 180°. Tai (3) stands almost vertically, turning only slightly to the back left.

Two white lily blossoms rise from the middle of the composition and turn towards the front.

In a previous section of this book, we compiled a number of methods on how to keep plants fresh longer. Here, a word about spurge — this is a plant which, when cut, secretes 'milk' in order to close the vessels and prevent drying out and bleeding. We, however, want to keep the vessels on the cut open. Therefore, we singe the cut with a candle or something similar and then place it immediately in water. The blossoms stay fresh longer when we pick off most of the leaves.

Possible variations include using orange tiger lilies or gleaming tiger lilies.

103

Plants   weeping willow branches *(Salix babylonica)*
three Chinese juniper branches
three tulips with leaves
Container   ceramic vase, anthracite glaze with white pattern

Tall, slender vases like these are especially well suited for the Suitai style when shin slants at an angle of more than 90°. Choose a suitable hana-kubari model and allow shin (1) and soe (2) to curve gently to the front right.

The balancing element, tai (3), is also formed by a weeping willow branch which, however, rises sharply upwards somewhat to the right.

The powerful blue-green juniper branches follow the direction and movement of the main line. The tulips as well, cut to different sizes, happily follow the path initiated by shin and soe.

Shildare Yanagi, the weeping willow, was a preferred ikebana material as far back as the fourteenth and fifteenth centuries. Even today the Japanese love the fine, graceful line it makes when blown by a soft breeze. Perhaps this has something to do with the East Asian mentality, with their flexibility and adaptability. Using these branches it is possible to create very sad themes (illustration IV) but very friendly and joyous ones too. In our ikebana, we have stressed certain things and through the use of circles, we have livened up the thin, long lines.

The friendly, happy feeling conveyed by our arrangement would be destroyed if we allowed the tulip leaves to hang tiredly over the rim. The leaves should look fresh for our Nageïre. For that reason we can cut them down to size or roll them up.

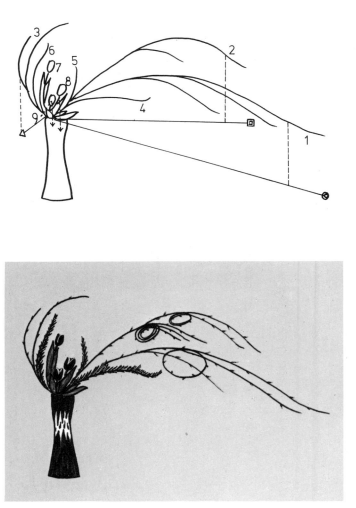

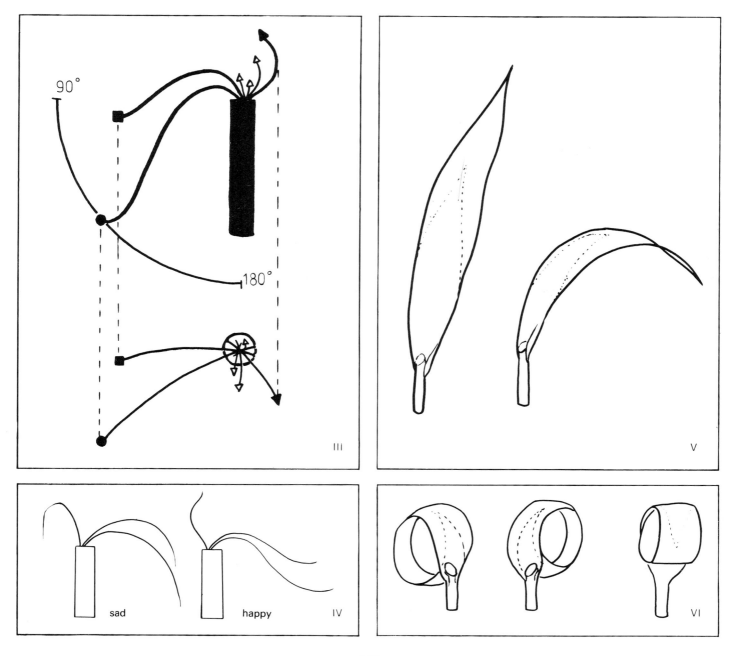

90°

180°

III

sad   happy   IV

V

VI

Plants two weigelia branches
five garnet roses
Container glazed, turquoise ceramic vase

The procedure for making the arrangement is once again divided into five steps. First, the shin branch is fixed onto the hana-kubari (1). It curves downwards at an angle of more than 90°. Soe (2) is fastened to shin in such a way that it has an upward direction, slanting somewhat to the back right. Tai (3) is made up of roses. A long rose not yet fully opened stands in the centre. The others graduated in size turn towards the observer.

If we leave a bit of the stem on the leaves, we can place them into the vase without difficulty thereby enlivening the centre of the composition.

With the help of the somewhat stronger, green-finished carnation wire, the front roses can be prevented from drooping their heads. Make sure, however, that the wire remains invisible.

To vary this style, the following branches are especially well suited — larch, birch, cotoneaster, spurge, spiraea or forsythia.

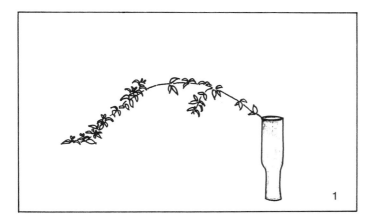

1

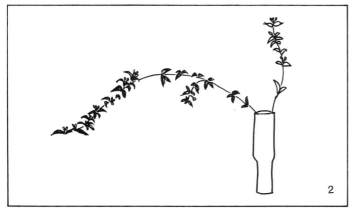

2

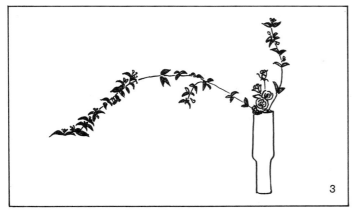

3

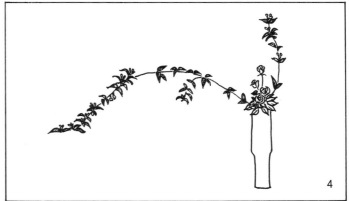

4

107

Plants   a gnarled goat willow branch with young sprouts
five daffodils
some asparagus fern
Container   cylindrical, blue-green glazed vase

Which element would you regard as shin, which as tai?
What does this arrangement mean to you?
Can you interpret this arrangement?

Plants   Virginia creepers
                  anemones
Container stone-shaped ceramic vase with small mouth

We have entitled this ikebana 'Contrast'.
  Take your time and consider it.
  Linger very quietly a quarter of an hour in front of your composition. Relax and observe it.

NAGEÏRE
CREATIVE STYLE

NAGEÏRE
CREATIVE STYLE

Plants   weeping willow
             yellow lilies
             orange carnations
Container 45-cm-high, brown ceramic vase with rough surface

Plants   broom
             chrysanthemums
Container bellied, brown ceramic vase

What is the relationship here between the three main lines and the vase?

   Give reasons for the deviation from the basic style.

   Compose yourself a Nageïre arrangement in a very high vase and observe how different proportions change the effect.

Broom is made up of many fine lines. In order to show these lines clearly, the shoots are bent in one direction. This is the natural shape of the bush. In this way, numerous different moods can be created.

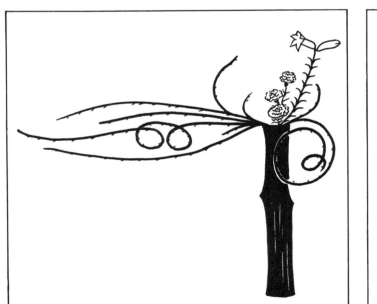

Plants   cornelian cherry *(Cornus mas)*
               salmon pink tulips
Container   a square vase and a rectangular tray
               Japanese ceramic, blue namako-glaze

The Futakabu-ike (two-group arrangement) is to be regarded as the foundation of this Moribana–Nageïre combination. The container includes a masculine part (okabu) and a feminine one (mekabu). In our arrangement, the okabu part is in the tray, while the mekabu part is contained in the vase. Both parts can be arranged to balance each other or modern social concepts can be brought into the composition.

Shin (1), towering upward, is placed in the basin bending slightly to the front right. Soe (2) strengthens the supporting gesture of shin, and remains somewhat in the background. In response to the main lines in the tray, tai (3) is placed in the vase curving towards the other half of the composition. A small cornelian cherry branch underscores the communication. Two tulips of different lengths are now arranged in the tray (5, 6) as tai-indicators. The tulips in the Nageïre (7) turn towards the Moribana.

Combination styles can also be created in two trays or in two vases of different heights. Three or more containers can also be used. There are no limits to the imagination.

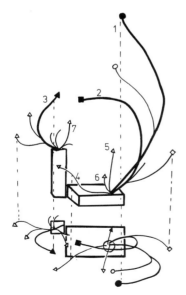

Plants   weeping willow
           three tulips
Container a combination of a container comprising a cylindrical
           light blue vase and a small bowl with the same glaze,
           which when placed on top of the vase forms a cup

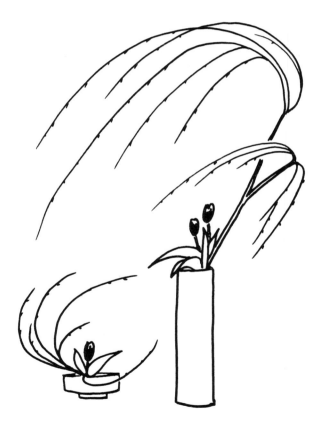

We have already gathered quite a bit of experience with weeping willows. With patience, we will be able to make all secondary branches move in the desired direction. If we vary this direction only slightly, the expression of the combination arrangement can be completely altered.

Birch and larch branches are also suitable for this ikebana style.

MODERN SHÔKA

What is Modern Shôka?

Firstly, we want to become acquainted with modern Shôka because it is technically and conceptually simpler than classical Shôka whose historical development we have already considered and which was conceived mainly for the tokonoma, or niche of honour, in Japanese rooms. Today's world and modern life often demand more striking arrangements and new containers. Ikebana has become known internationally since World War 2 and has incorporated many influences from all over the world. For this reason, a new Shôka style was developed at the Ikenobô Culture Institute in 1954 which is less strict and allows the arranger more freedom without abandoning the traditional lines.

For *Gendai-Shoka*, today's Shôka, usually three different plants are used. For this reason we also speak of *Sanshu-ike Shôka*, 'three material Shôka'. If two plants are used, we speak of *Nishu-ike,* and for one, *Isshu-ike.*

Modern Shôka styles

Whereas classical Shôka prescribes the use of traditional containers, numerous different kinds of vases can be employed for modern Shôka. In spite of this, the container must match the ikebana style. A suitable arrangement can also be created for an interesting cup.

We differentiate the following three styles of modern Shôka:

Style	Characteristics	Container
SHIN-Style	This style has a slender rather austere appearance	Mostly tall cups or vases, figs. 1, 2, 4, 8, 9, 11
GYÔ-Style	This arrangement has a somewhat broader design than the Shin-style	Less slender cups and chalices, figs. 2, 3, 5, 6, 8, 9, 10, 11, 12
SÔ-Style	This style is broad and lively. It is not ascetic but rather sensuous, open and worldly	Broad cups, bowls with feet or wide basins, figs. 5, 6, 7, 10, 12, 13, 14, 15

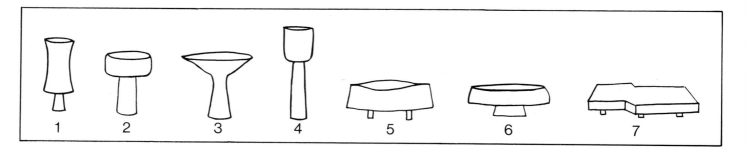

114

Flower Holders for Modern Shôka
Kenzan with adjustable metal sidepiece (top left)
Kenzan with adjustable height (top middle)
Shippô made of 1–3 rings (top right)
Various kinds of kenzan (below)

**Symbols for base positions
in Modern Shôka**

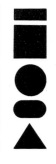

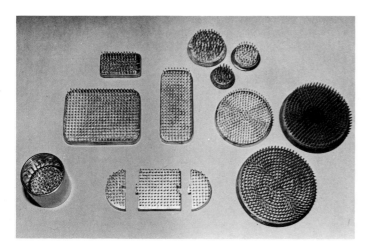

Symbols representing Modern Shôka

We are also trying to represent modern Shôka graphically and expect thereby to give students greater clarity concerning the structure of the arrangement. Perhaps the schematic representation can be compared to musical notes in which all nuances of interpretation are not given either, although the artist is given a survey of the composition and its harmony.

Just as we have done all along, here too, we have drawn a diagram which is seen from the front, and another one, which is seen from above. The five main parts of modern Shôka are represented with the symbols already used for shin, soe and tai, and the two new ones for dô (oval) and sugata naoshi (rectangle).

115

SHIN ●	means 'truth' just as in Moribana and Nageïre. Shin, the largest and longest line, determines the character of the arrangement and is approximately two to three times as long as the diameter and height of the container together.
SOE ■	means help and support just as in Moribana and Nageïre. The soe branch is the second most important line and usually slants at a 45° angle towards the back. It is about two-thirds as long as shin.
TAI ▲	means body just as in Moribana and Nageïre and often turns towards the front at an angle of 45°. The length is approximately one-third that of shin.
DÔ ⬭	means trunk and is arranged next to tai in the centre of the composition. Dô can attain a size of almost half that of shin.
SUGATA NAOSHI ▬	is a form improving line. (*Sugata* means form, external view, and *Naoshi* means to correct, improve, beautify.)

What do we mean by 'base position'?

In Shôka (Seika) and Rikka exact rules have developed concerning how the stems of plants are to be arranged in the flower holder, so that a well-balanced spatial effect is achieved. It is important that the whole composition grows as if from one stem and only then separates into individual lines so that one has the feeling that the whole power of the arrangement originates in the base and rises upwards.

In modern Shôka, tai is usually placed furthest towards the front. By front we mean, as we have meant up until now, the side of the arrangement facing the observer or arranger. Then dô, shin, soe and sugata naoshi follow. In special cases this suggested sequence does not have to be followed.

How to bend branches.

1. Press the branch against your thumbs.
2. Cut into the branch up to one-third of diameter, then bend gently.
3. Cut the branch and insert a piece of wood (for further explanation see pages 84 and 85)

1

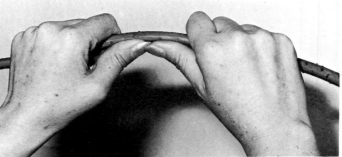

2

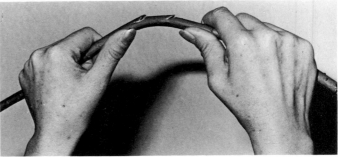

3

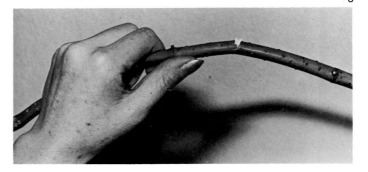

Plants lupins
cotoneaster
rape
Container ceramic cup, black matt glaze

This summerlike arrangement comprises exclusively plants growing wild in nature which we brought back from a walk. The lovely blossoming lupin should of course serve as shin setting the tone of the composition with its lovely airy freshness. The golden rape flower, which blossoms in the early spring in Japan and is used for the Festival of Young Girls on 3 March, adds a cheerful fresh contrast. In this way the somewhat severe lines of this slender composition are softened. By having the branches spread out approximately 10 cm above the rim of the container, we create the impression of a summer plant.

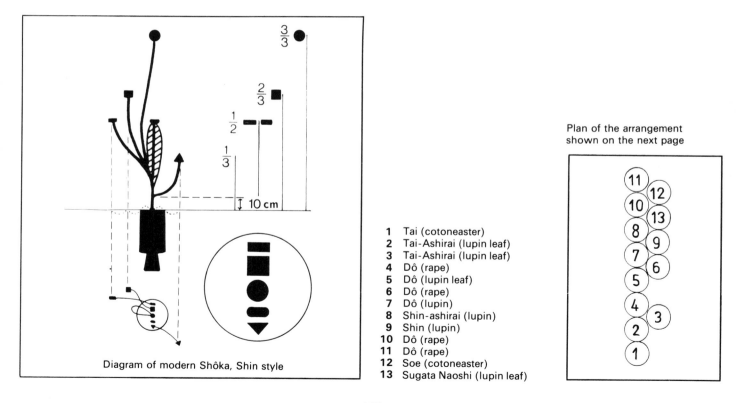

Diagram of modern Shôka, Shin style

1 Tai (cotoneaster)
2 Tai-Ashirai (lupin leaf)
3 Tai-Ashirai (lupin leaf)
4 Dô (rape)
5 Dô (lupin leaf)
6 Dô (rape)
7 Dô (lupin)
8 Shin-ashirai (lupin)
9 Shin (lupin)
10 Dô (rape)
11 Dô (rape)
12 Soe (cotoneaster)
13 Sugata Naoshi (lupin leaf)

Plan of the arrangement
shown on the next page

117

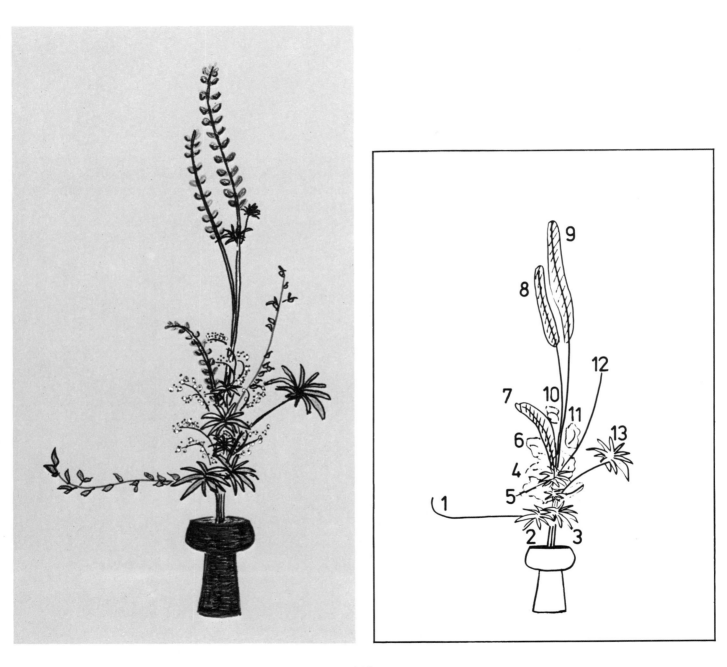

Plants   foxglove
             calla leaves
             amaryllis
Container white glazed ceramic cup

This modern composition also gives an impression of summer warmth. Here, we have combined a typical garden flower, the foxglove, with an amaryllis which in colour tone matches exactly. The five large leaves of the calla radiate strength and fullness.

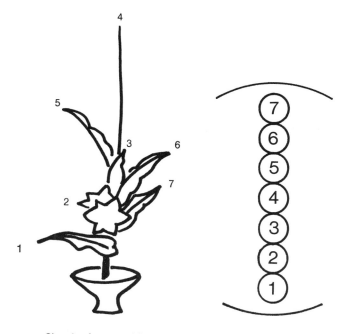

Sketch of composition   Plan in kenzan

Plants   seven small-blossomed sunflowers *(Helianthus rigidus)*
two dark blue irises
three forsythia branches *(Forsythia intermedia spektabilis)*
Container tall, light blue ceramic cup

The sunflowers are arranged as shin (10) and shin-ashirai (9). Soe comprises a sunflower stem (11) and a branch (12) and turns on a slant towards the back. Dô is formed in the following manner — an iris blossom is placed in the centre (7) and the sunflowers (5, 6, 8) are placed in front of shin. Flowers (4) and (3) are placed all the way to the front as tai-ashirai. Between (4) and (5), we now insert the forsythia branches as tai (1, 2). An iris leaf making an elegant curve towards the back is sugata-naoshi.

In this way we maintain a very noble Shôka-base. We conceal the woody tai branches (1, 2) between the flower stems (4) and (3) so as not to break up the summerlike green of the base.

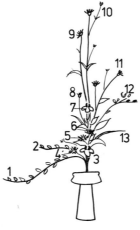

Sketch of composition

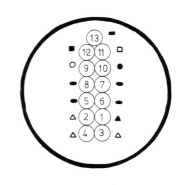

Base position in kenzan

LESSON 45

Plants Flowering currant branches *(Ribes sanguineum)*
two sansevieria leaves
three red roses
Container square, black ceramic vessel with feet

MODERN SHÔKA
GYÔ–STYLE
Sanshu-ike

1 Dô (rose)
2 Dô (rose)
3 Dô (sansevieria)
4 Tai (blackcurrant branch)
5 Dô (sansevieria)
6 Dô (rose)
7 Shin (blackcurrant branch)
8 Soe (blackcurrant branch)
9 Sugata Naoshi (blackcurrant branch)

The flowering currant branches are still bare. As a contrast to them we use, just as for each winter composition, some green from house plants or evergreen branches. In Japan we often employ fir branches, symbolic of long life. Three red roses alone would not be strong enough to form dô, so the sturdy leaves of the sansevieria come in handy.

Sketch of composition

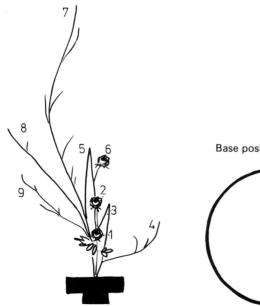

Base position in kenzan

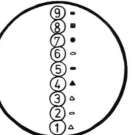

121

Plants   seven montbretias *(Crocosmia aurea)*
             five pincushion flowers *(Scabiosa caucasica)*
             broom *(Cytisus)*
Container light blue ceramic cup

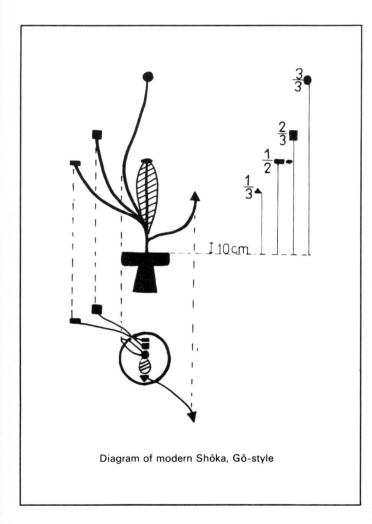

Diagram of modern Shôka, Gô-style

The distinctive characteristic of the montbretia is its numerous delicate and exceptionally graceful leaves. In this arrangement we try to emphasize the special delicacy of line. For this reason, we choose as second plant the gentle buds of the scabiosa which also harmonize well with the montbretia as far as colour is concerned.

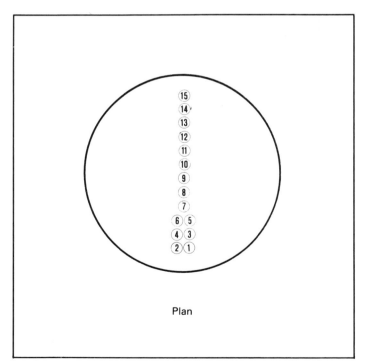

Plan

The kind of broom used here adapts well to the harmony of the lines. The stems are to be arranged in two rows as close to each other as possible on a large kenzan so that the base matches the elegance of the arrangement itself.

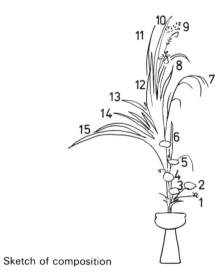

Sketch of composition

1, 2	Tai (pincushion flower)
3, 4, 5, 6	Dô (pincushion flower)
7	Shin-Ashirai (broom)
8	Shin-Ashirai (leaves of montbretia)
9, 10	Shin (leaves and blossoms of montbretia)
11, 12	Shin-Ashirai (leaves and blossoms of montbretia)
13, 14	Soe-Ashirai (leaves and blossoms of montbretia)
15	Soe (leaves and blossoms of montbretia)

LESSON 47

Plants   guelder roses
              Allium giganteum
              tiger lilies
Container hand turned, brown ceramic bowl

1 Tai-Saki (front Tai; guelder rose)
2 Tai (guelder rose)
3 Dô (allium)
4 Dô (allium)
5 Dô (tiger lily)
6 Dô (tiger lily)
7 Shin-Mae-Ashirai (front Shin filler; allium)
8 Shin (guelder rose)
9 Shin-Ushiro-Ashirai (rear Shin filler; guelder rose)
10 Soe (guelder rose)
11 Sugata Naoshi (guelder rose)

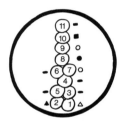

Base position in kenzan

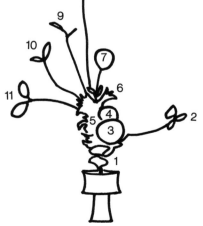

Sketch of composition

124

Plants   sunflowers
             philodendron leaves *(Monstera)*
             bleached wisteria rolled into a spiral
Container low, black ceramic cup
Title   'Goodbye Summer'

We conceal a sunflower behind the large leaves, two withered ones mark shin. Small supports have to be used for the heavy flower heads. In this case a very large, heavy kenzan is indispensable. An attempt at a farewell dance is portrayed here by bleached wisteria vines which have been artificially rolled in spirals.

Sugata naoshi has been omitted since soe already makes a strong enough impression.

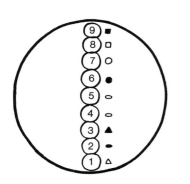

Base position in kenzan

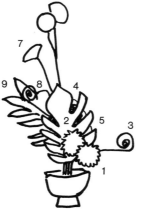

Sketch of composition

125

Plants   white thorn branches
             mulleins
             liatris
Container ceramic cup, with blue-grey stripes
Title   'July'

If you find very tall mulleins, use them as shin choosing the slender shin style. As a contrast to the yellow of the mulleins, we have chosen the purple of the liatris.

Sketch of composition

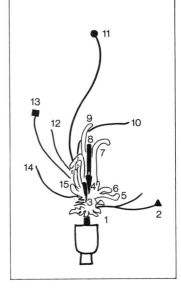

Base position in kenzan

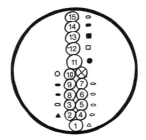

Plants	willow branches *(Salix daphnoides)*
	pink roses
	small, white chrysanthemums
Container	Suiban, black, ceramic water basin

1 Dô (chrysanthemum leaf)
2 Dô (chrysanthemum)
3 Dô (rose)
4, 5 Tai (willows)
6 Dô (rose)
7 Dô (chrysanthemum)
8 Shin-Ashirai, front (willow branches)
9 Shin-Ashirai (willow branches)
10 Shin (willow branches)
11 Shin-Ashirai, rear (willow branches)
12 Soe-Ashirai (willows)
13 Soe (willows)
14 Soe-Ashirai (willows)
15 Sugata Naoshi (willows)

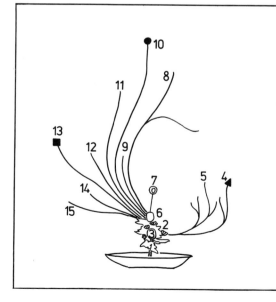

127

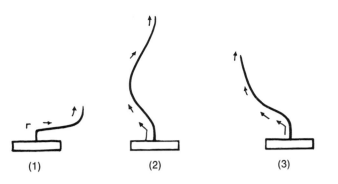

(1)   (2)   (3)

Plants	New Zealand flax *(Phormium tenax)*
	roses
Container	Nijû, double-bamboo container

Bending the willow branches is very important in this line composition. As you know from previous lessons these branches are especially easy to bend and you already know the methods used to bend them properly. Firstly, the tai branch is bent sharply and then turned upwards (1). For shin and shin-ashirai, first a large outward curve is made before forming the upward curve (2). Soe is, as shown in the sketch, bent outwards (3).

This arrangement was made by Professor Koushû Murata (Tokyo/Yokohama), my honoured teacher. It should show the numerous variations made possible by modern Shôka. Before attemtping 'creative Shôka', one should first have gained enough experience in working with more restricted styles.

Diagram of modern Shôka, Sô Style

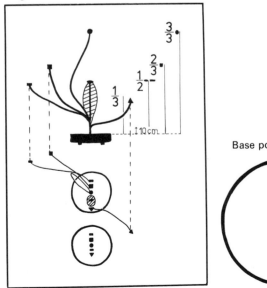

Base position in kenzan

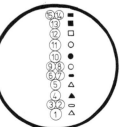

128

MODERN SHÔKA
SÔ STYLE
Sanshu-ike
Futakabu-ike
(two-group arrangement)

Plants	a large great burnet *(Sanguisorba officinalis)*
	decorative grass *(Miscanthus vittatus)*
	(Rudbekia)
Container	black, matt water basin (Suiban)

The Futakabu-ike, a two group arrangement, is especially attractive here just as in Rikka, Moribana, and Nageïre. It comprises a masculine and a feminine part (okabu and mekabu).

The burnet with its dark brown 'buttons' grows in swamps and goes very well with the decorative grass and the yellow blossoms of the daisy.

The white striped miscanthus is, in both parts of the composition, the most important material for dô.

In the mekabu part of the arrangement, the smaller one,

lines 1 and 2 form tai and tai-ashirai and lines 3, 4 and 5 form dô.

In the okabu, or larger masculine section, 3 is dô, 4 is shin-ashirai at the back, 5 is shin, 6 is shin-ashirai at the front, 7 is soe, 2 is sugata naoshi, and 1 is tai-za (indication of tai).

To vary the composition, you can also employ Japanese pampas grass or *Miscanthus sinensis* and asters. Reed-mace (commonly, the bulrush) together with hollyhocks, chrysanthemums or irises are well suited to this style.

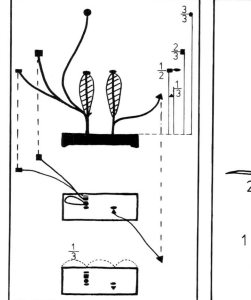
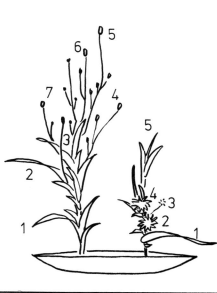

CLASSICAL SHÔKA

What is Classical Shôka?

Shôka or *Seika* means the same as the word *Ikebana,* namely 'to arrange flowers', 'living flowers' and 'flowers that have been put in their best light'. Since about the seventeenth century, it has been contrasted with the complicated and luxurious Rikka. Due to the influence of Zen-Buddhism and the related tea ceremony, this simple, slick and delicate style of ikebana arose. Even the style of the containers became simpler and clearer. During the golden age of Seika (Shôka) from about the seventeenth to nineteenth centuries, various styles were created and new schools formed.

Today as well, Shôka, like other classical ikebana styles, enjoys great popularity although a great deal of time is needed to learn it. The most important schools which still teach classical Seika today are Ikenobô, Koryû, Ryûseiha, Mishô and Enshû.

Many modern people today are enchanted by the simplicity of the classical containers and gladly submit to the strict rules concerning containers for classical Shôka. The traditional bamboo containers, the bronze vases or water basins (Suiban), the various moon-shaped containers (Tsuki) as well as the ship-style flower holders (Fune) are now becoming increasingly popular outside Japan as well.

But even though the use of containers is exactly prescribed and there are strict rules governing choice, combination, and arrangement of plants, no classical Shôka is exactly like another. In each composition, the creative abilities of the individual combine with the traditional rules to form an arrangement. These rules are acknowledged as non-individualistic or supra-individualistic.

Classical Shôka styles and containers

The characteristics of various Shôka styles are known to us from modern Shôka. The Shin style is slender and formal, the Gyô style somewhat broader, while the Sô style curves well out to the sides or sometimes even downwards. The following is a table showing containers which can be used for classical Shôka styles.

Style	Container			
Shin style	Zundo (bamboo)	Zundo (wood)	Ichimonji (bronze)	Shikaimi (bronze)

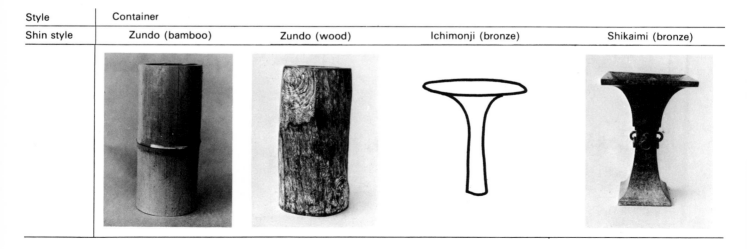

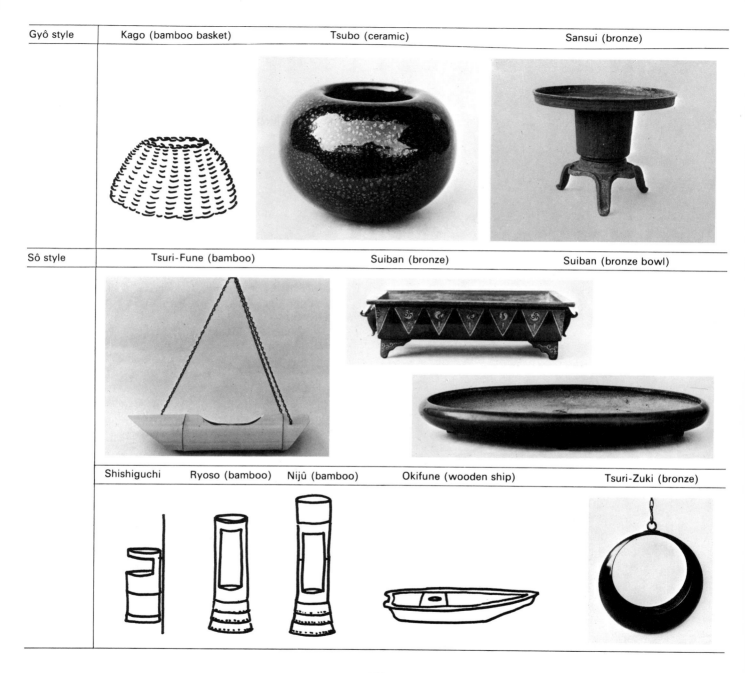

| Gyô style | Kago (bamboo basket) | Tsubo (ceramic) | Sansui (bronze) |

| Sô style | Tsuri-Fune (bamboo) | Suiban (bronze) | Suiban (bronze bowl) |

| Shishiguchi | Ryoso (bamboo) | Nijû (bamboo) | Okifune (wooden ship) | Tsuri-Zuki (bronze) |

1	3
	4
2	5

KADAI - tables and trays

1 Tray made of root
2 Adjustable trays
3 KUMOGATA (cloud-shaped trays)
4 Carved wooden table (50 cm)
5 Small, carved wooden table

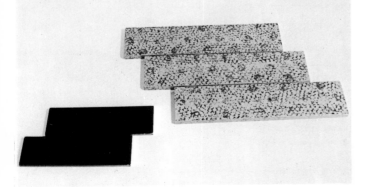

132

Hana-kubari for Shôka

The illustration shows how you yourself can make a hana-kubari from a branch having a diameter of approximately 1 or 1.5 cm. One method is to take a straight piece cutting it so that it is longer than the diameter of the container, tying it on one side with flower wire or bast, then splitting it with a knife or scissors and clamping it carefully into place in the container. The other method is to look for a forked branch whose angle matches the thickness of the stems used in the arrangement.

Various Kubari positions

For all cylindrical flower and water containers a hana-kubari (wooden fork flower holder) is used. It is clamped against the sides of the container at about 2 cm under the rim. For this reason, we use branches which are quite elastic to form the kubari, for example those from the willow or dogwood trees

Figure 1 A   Side of container
         B   Kubari
         C   Tomegi (locking wood)
         D   Stems of branches and flowers

We use this kubari position mostly for those Shôka arrangements in which the base projects vertically out of the centre of the container (Ikenobô, Saga-School). After all branches and flowers are in place, an elastic piece of branch is clamped behind the flowers against the sides of the container. In this way, the arrangement is held tightly in position. This device is called in Japanese a *Tomegi*.

Figure II (overleaf)
If the base of the Seika slants sharply to the left, this kubari position is used (Koryû, Saga, Mishô Schools and others).

Figure III
For Seika arrangements slanting slightly to the left (Koryû, Saga, Mishô Schools and others).

Figure IV
Kubari position for Seika slanting to the right (Koryû, Saga and Mishô Schools and others).

Figure V
Kubari position for Seika leaning sharply to the right or for a horizontal style (Koryû, Saga, Mishô Schools and others).

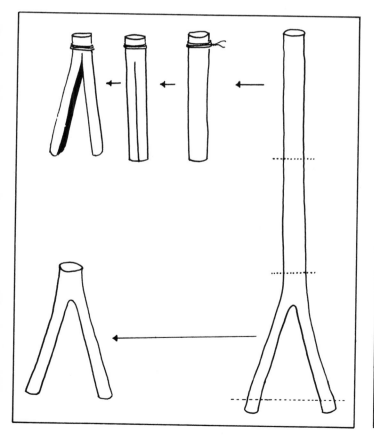

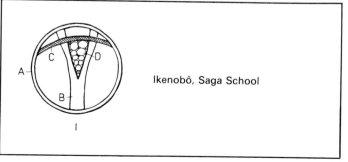

Ikenobô, Saga School

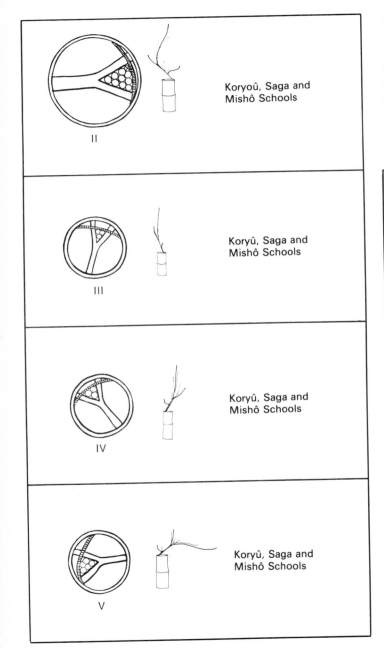

	Koryoû, Saga and Mishô Schools
II	

	Koryû, Saga and Mishô Schools
III	

	Koryû, Saga and Mishô Schools
IV	

	Koryû, Saga and Mishô Schools
V	

How to cut branches for Shôka

For all kinds of Seika (Shôka) in which the base of the arrangement stands vertically on the bottom of the container, the branches and flowers are cut straight across, and sometimes notches are made at the bottom with the scissors or with a knife (1). If, however, the stems lean against the sides of the container they are cut on a slant so that they fit snugly.

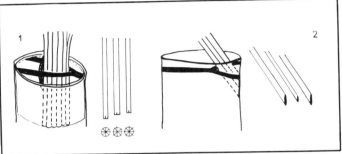

The use of the shippô

For Seika styles in shallow bowls or basins, most ikebana schools use a metal shippô, a flower holder without needles. The drawings show how wooden branches and soft flower stems and leaves are arranged in the spaces. By using small pieces of wood or several short, additional

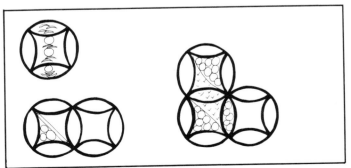

stems, a stable upright position is obtained. Today, some schools allow the use of kenzans for classical Shôka as well.

Construction models for classical Shôka

In classical Shôka the base arrangement is of great importance. For this reason we are presenting in the following drawings four models on how to put together a complete arrangement or part of one.

Each classical Shôka comprises three main elements:

Shin   ●
Soe   ■
Tai   ▲

To symbolize these elements we are using the same solid circles, squares and triangles as before.

A series of fillers support the main elements. To symbolize these ashirai we are using the signs which indicate the main elements but we are not filling them in. A shin-ashirai will, for example, be symbolized by an open circle. Fillers which stand in front of the main line are called *Mae-Ashirai,* and those which stand behind the main line are called *Ushiro-Ashirai.*

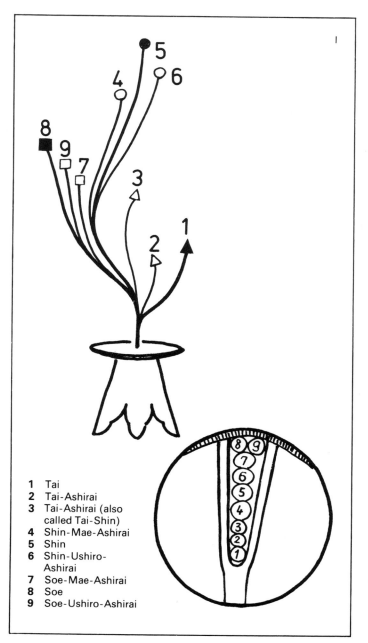

1 Tai
2 Tai-Ashirai
3 Tai-Ashirai (also called Tai-Shin)
4 Shin-Mae-Ashirai
5 Shin
6 Shin-Ushiro-Ashirai
7 Soe-Mae-Ashirai
8 Soe
9 Soe-Ushiro-Ashirai

This Shôka is made up of three groups of lines. The shin group comprises three branches, so does the soe group, while the tai group contains three flowers.

The individual lines are provided with numbers so that their position in the kubari can be exactly determined. The first branch to be placed in the flower holder is tai, the second is the short tai-ashirai, etc. (Figure 1).

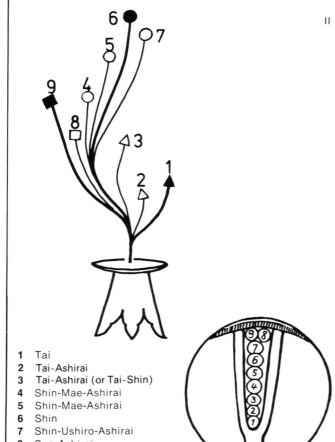

1 Tai
2 Tai-Ashirai
3 Tai-Ashirai (or Tai-Shin)
4 Shin-Mae-Ashirai
5 Shin-Mae-Ashirai
6 Shin
7 Shin-Ushiro-Ashirai
8 Soe-Ashirai
9 Soe

Another variation is presented here as a model. Once again, the tai group is made up of three flowers, but the shin group has four branches and the soe group for this reason has only two. From the diagram alone, one cannot distinguish which of the lines must be arranged in the back, and which in the front in order to obtain an elegant spatial effect. However, by comparing the numbers of the lines with those of the base arrangement, everything becomes clear.

Here, only the tai group of the two previous arrangements has been drawn. Base position and length proportions within this part of the composition become clear. This model is valid when tai is made of three flowers.

III

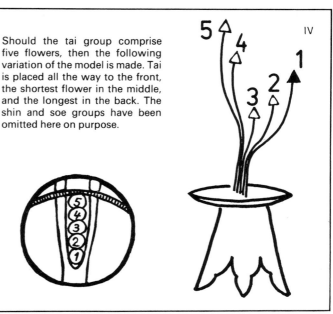

Should the tai group comprise five flowers, then the following variation of the model is made. Tai is placed all the way to the front, the shortest flower in the middle, and the longest in the back. The shin and soe groups have been omitted here on purpose.

IV

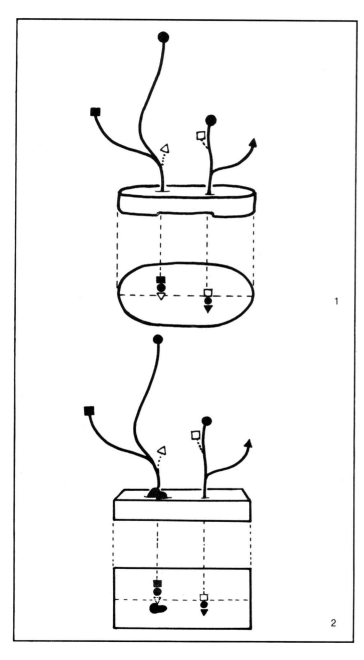

1

2

What is Shôka-Futakabu-ike?

In today's Shôka (Gendai-Shôka) as well as in classical Shôka, two group arrangements are recognized. They are derived from Rikka-Futakabu-ike which was cultivated very early.

The three most important kinds of Shôka-Futakabu-ike are Gyodô-ike, Suiriku-ike and Niju-ike.

Figure 1
Gyodô-ike, the fish way arrangement
Gyodô-ike is a two group composition containing only water plants arranged in a container. It is derived from the Rikka-Futakabu-ike. The shin-soe section is the masculine part (okabu), the tai section, the feminine part (mekabu). Using these two groups the spatial depth of a water landscape is created.

Figure 2
Suiriku-ike, the water-land-arrangement
Suiriku-ike is a two group Shôka in which the masculine part is made up of land plants and the feminine one of water plants. A stone placed near the masculine part indicates the land behind it.

Figure 3
Nijû-ike, the double arrangement
Nijû-ike is a two group Shôka in which both groups are arranged one above the other in a two level container. In this way either the larger part can be on top or vice versa.

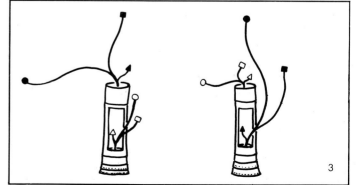

3

137

Plants   gladiolas with beautiful leaves
Container   Zundo made of bamboo

With a bit of skill you can even make one of these containers yourself by taking a 30-cm-long piece of tree trunk and hollowing it out from the top by about 10–15 cm, then inserting a water container of copper or zinc-plate. This kind of container can also be made out of a piece of iron piping or ceramic.

Note the proportions shown in the illustrations. Here again, shin: soe: tai maintain the same proportions 3: 2: 1. Here, the height of the container is the same as that of tai.

First hold the flowers and leaves in front of you and observe their lines. Only then decide whether you want to use soe at the right, as here, or to the left. Use a forked twig which opens towards the back as kubari, and cut a tomegi out of the same piece of wood. First place the tai group at the bottom of the container through the kubari so that it bends somewhat towards the left (figure II). Cut the leaves and stems straight across under water.

The following soe group (figure III) now bends to the right but only very slightly.

The shin line is placed beside this, its movement harmonizes with soe and balances tai (figure IV).

I   II   III   IV

Plants   two branches of Canadian amelanchier
          (*Amelanchier canadensis*)
          one tulip
Container Japanese bronze container Ichimonji ('one line')
          with large calm water surface

Begin with the tai group, the tulip and the leaves, placing the shin branch vertically in the kubari, and finally soe facing back left.

This arrangement shows how little is needed to conjure up spring in the home. Even a container like this one could be made by an enthusiastic potter.

Other possible plant combinations:
Two branches and a daffodil.
Three flowers such as irises or gladiolas.
Three leaves such as African hemp or aspidistra.
Two white lilies and a rose, etc.

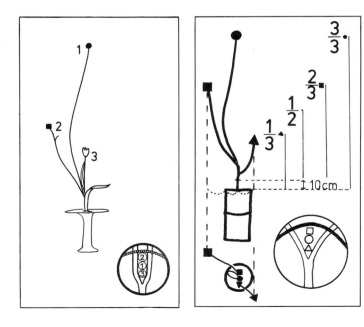

Plants   liatris
          peony
Container   Shikaimi ('four seas waves') of the Ikenobô
            School, bronze, a black laquered wooden
            table serves as kadai

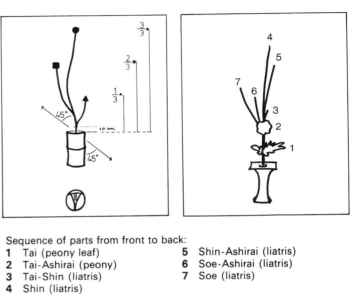

Sequence of parts from front to back:
1 Tai (peony leaf)
2 Tai-Ashirai (peony)
3 Tai-Shin (liatris)
4 Shin (liatris)

5 Shin-Ashirai (liatris)
6 Soe-Ashirai (liatris)
7 Soe (liatris)

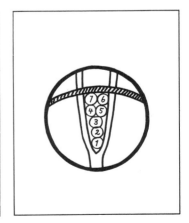

140

Plants   hornbeam branches
Container   Zundo vase of bamboo

Arrangement by Shishû Kobayashi, a master of the Saga School. According to the teachings of this school, the parts of the composition are designed in the following way:

Tai (style determining) is the longest branch
Yô (style supporting) the middle line
Tome (style terminating) the shortest

The special feature in this composition is that Yô flows downward. That is why this style is called Yô-Nagashi. Cut branches on a slant.

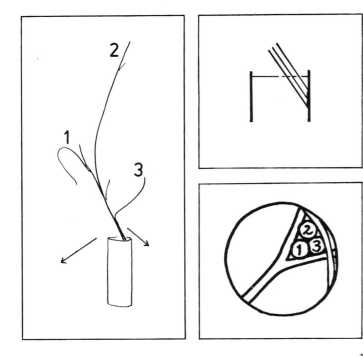

Plants   spindle tree *(Euonymus alatus)*
Container Zundo vase of bamboo

Arrangement by Master Shishû Kobayashi, Saga School.
The harmonious lines of this Isshu-ike arrangement make a
striking appearance in spite of the simplicity of the branch
and container, or perhaps just because of it.

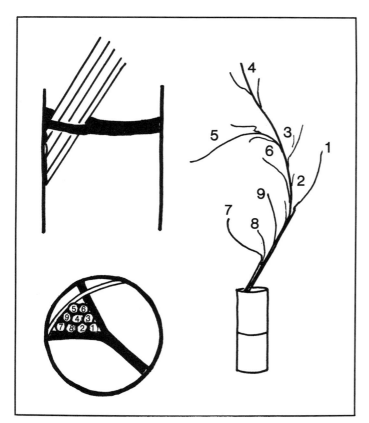

Plants   cypress branches
             small chrysanthemums
Container   Japanese Ogenchô of bronze

The Gyô style, curving further out over the rim of the container, has a more striking effect than the more formal Shin style.

In addition to the parts arranged in a row in figure I, several other fillers will be added to shin and soe.

Soe faces to the back left, and tai to the front right.

143

Plants	plum branches *(Prunus mume)*
	camellia *(Camellia japonica)*
Container	Noshigata, bronze vase

This masterful arrangement was created by Professor Kashô Kaneko, the great Ikenobô teacher and President of the Ikenobô Ikebana Society in Tokyo, for an exhibition in the National Museum Tokyo.

The fragile blossoms of the plum branches are used for shin and soe, while camellia branches with blossoms form tai.

Variations

Spring:
Blossoming sloe branches and daffodils with many leaves
Blossoming white thorn branches with tulips
Summer:
Flowering currant branches and irises
Corn and tiger-lilies
Autumn:
Maple and chrysanthemums
Plum branches and asters
Winter:
Mountain pine and small chrysanthemums
Yew tree branches and daffodils

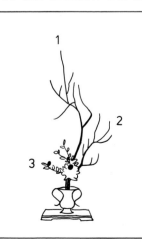

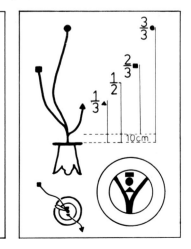

Plants   jasmine *(Jasminum odoratissimum)*
             gerbera with leaves
Container Suiban, shallow ceramic bowl

This composition can be arranged in a shippô, as shown at the beginning of this course. Today, however, even traditional schools allow the use of the flower holder (kenzan). We are using a kenzan in our example.

For this reason, here too, the shin branch can be placed first, just as in Moribana (figure II).

This branch was, however, first brought into harmony with the other two groups as far as contours, masses, and proportions are concerned (figure I).

The soe branch slants to the back left, while the tai line faces to the front right.

When using a kenzan and a shallow bowl, the base of the arrangement must be slender, rise straight upwards, and not begin branching outwards before about 10 cm.

I   II   III   IV

Plants   day-lily *(Hemerocallis)*
Container   Suiban, ancient Japanese water basin in bronze

Our students have always found great pleasure in this style. It is arranged in a wide-mouthed bowl (hirokuchi) as a one group arrangement rising upwards from the base (hitokabu-ike) using only one kind of plant. This style is thus called Hiro-kuchi-hitokabu-isshu-ike.

The day-lily has numerous clearly curving leaves. For this reason it is especially well suited for Shôka and Rikka.

The leaves have to be handled with special care and cut with exceptionally sharp scissors.

English irises *(Iris ciphiodes anglica)* can also be used in place of the day-lilies if they have enough good leaves.

This composition can be arranged in a shippô, or in a kenzan which has been placed in the middle of the container.

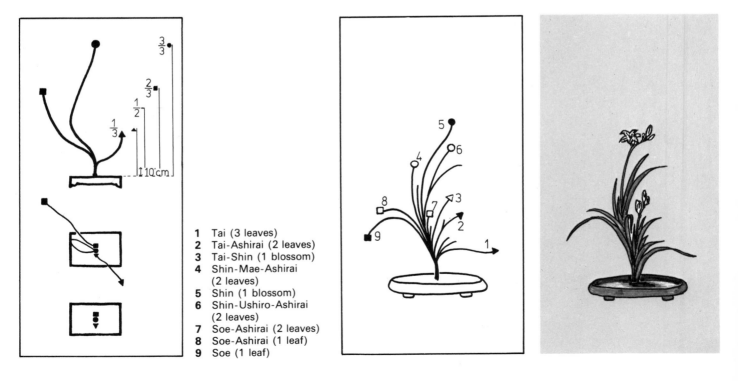

1 Tai (3 leaves)
2 Tai-Ashirai (2 leaves)
3 Tai-Shin (1 blossom)
4 Shin-Mae-Ashirai
   (2 leaves)
5 Shin (1 blossom)
6 Shin-Ushiro-Ashirai
   (2 leaves)
7 Soe-Ashirai (2 leaves)
8 Soe-Ashirai (1 leaf)
9 Soe (1 leaf)

Plants   hornbeam branches
           iris *(Iris japonica)*
Container Japanese bronze bowl with feet on a cloud-
           shaped wooden tray (kumogata-kadai)

We recommend that you make a copy of this masterful arrangement by Professor Kashô Kaneko. When doing so, enjoy the contrast between the gnarled branch and the smooth, lance-shaped iris leaves. With little expense, the mood at the side of a pond has been captured, while displaying the different bearings of plants belonging to various floral communities.

Several well chosen rocks placed in the water indicate land.

Usually a fully opened blossom is placed at the very top of an iris composition in summer, and in spring open flowers are kept at the bottom while a few fresh leaves supported by one or more buds set the tone. In autumn, on the other hand, to set the tone, one may use leaves which have turned yellow or have been eaten away by insects, or whose lines are no longer so lively.

This Futakabu-ike is a Suiriku-ike (water–land–arrangement) like the one we described in the introduction to this course.

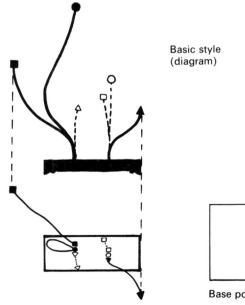

Basic style
(diagram)

Variation
(mirror
image)

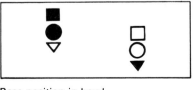

Base position in bowl

LESSON 63

SHÔKA
SÔ STYLE
Futakabu-ike
Gyodô-ike
Fish Way Arrangement

Plants   rush, Chinese reed *(Miscanthus sinensis)*
          iris
Container Suiban, Japanese ceramic basin

Gyodô-ike is composed exclusively of water plants, as we have shown in the introduction to this course. The rear, masculine group comprises rushes and Chinese reeds. The right front group (mekabu) is composed only of irises.

In the sketch below, we have drawn individually the mekabu parts in the sequence in which they are placed in the kenzan or shippô.

Why have we included this modern Shôka composition in a course for classical Shôka? Although the materials have been arranged in a simple, modern ceramic bowl instead of in a classical container, they themselves are classical and have been arranged in a traditional way which has been used since ancient times, even though several lines may be more in keeping with today's feeling for nature. For us, this ikebana is just as 'classical' as a Beethoven symphony performed in a modern concert hall by young musicians on instruments manufactured in this century.

Possible variations

Practice making a Gyodô-ike using other marsh plants or floating plant leaves like reeds, calla, reed-mace (bulrush), lotus, water-lilies or king cups.

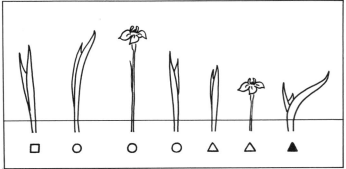

148

Plants   cotoneaster
             dahlias
             gladiolas
Ceramic   Nijû-giri, Japanese bamboo container
             with two openings

For this container, which you can also make yourself from a thick piece of bamboo, two different kinds of double arrangements are known in Japan. In the usual one, Nijû-ike (left) the upper part of the arrangement is the larger and the lower one the smaller. In the Nijû-tachinobori (right) the lower portion is more important. First, we cut a kubari to size for both sections of the container as explained in the introduction to this course.

The composition is arranged from front to back according to the sequence displayed in the composition sketch.

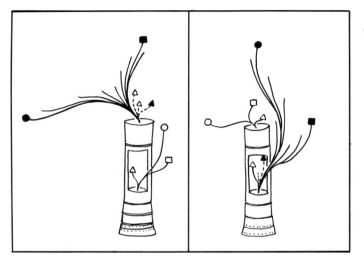

Upper section of the Nijû-Giri:
1 Tai (dahlia with buds and leaf)
2 Shin-Ashirai (cotoneaster branches)
3 Shin (cotoneaster)
4 Shin-Ashirai (cotoneaster)
5 Soe-Ashirai (cotoneaster)
6 Soe (cotoneaster)
7 Soe-Ushiro-Ashirai (cotoneaster)

Lower section of the Nijû-Giri:
1 Tai (gladiola leaves)
2 Tai-Shin (gladiola blossom)
3 Shin (two gladiola leaves)
4 Soe (two gladiola leaves)
5 Soe-Ushiro-Ashirai (gladiola leaf)

Plants   juniper
chrysanthemums
gerbera
Container Nijû-giri, double bamboo vase

Composition sketch of
upper arrangement

Base position of upper
arrangement

Composition sketch of
lower arrangement

Base position of lower
arrangement

Plants   sweet Williams *(Dianthus barbatus)*
            Celastrus orbiculatus
Container Mangetsu, Japanese full moon container
            bronze

This classical full moon container is used in the Ikenobô School. The Saga School also employs moon-shaped containers which are open at one point of the circle. They are called half moon containers *(Hangetsu)*.

We know a boat builder who makes very beautiful full moon containers out of plywood, coating them with black boat lacquer so that they remain waterproof for quite a long time. Potters too, including hobby potters among our Ikebana students, have made very useful moon-shaped containers.

In Japan such arrangements are hung in the Tokonoma (the niche of honour in Japanese homes). This ikebana arrangement should be hung at about eye level. Even in apartments decorated in modern European style, this moon composition has a charming effect. Since it doesn't take up any room and is relatively flat, it is well suited to small rooms such as halls and entrances. This style container always shows few and simple plants to their best advantage.

The Tai group comprises five sweet Williams, and the other two groups are made of only celastrus branches whose coloured berries match well.

Variations

Other plants such as Virginia creeper, birch and weeping willow can be used with flowers whose colour and form match well with the main material and surroundings.

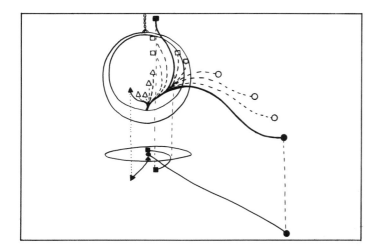

151

Plants   Virginia creeper *(Parthenocissus quinquefolia)*
           Michaelmas daisy *(Aster amellus)*
Container Tsuri-fune, hanging bamboo ship

Since Japan is an island country, the ship as a symbol plays an important role. For five hundred years the good wishes of those remaining home through the use of flower arrangements in ship style containers accompanied ships on their voyages. Since that time certain compositions are called Takara-bune (treasure filled ship).

Figure I shows a departing ship (defune) and figure II an arriving one. When the bow points to the left, it signifies a departing ship, and when it points to the right, an arriving one (irifune).

The ship arrangement hangs away from the wall like a hanging flower lamp just as in a Japanese tokonoma. The empty space around it symbolizes the sea.

Tai and tai-ashirai are again represented by flowers in order to give the composition a central focal point.

Shin and soe are composed of tendrils.

The special feature of the Tsuri-fune arrangement is its unusual fourth line. Here, made concrete by a tendril, it represents the rudder (ro).

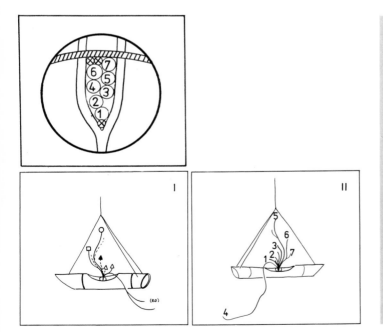

CLASSICAL SHÔKA
SÔ STYLE
Tsuri-Fune
Hanging Ship

CLASSICAL SHÔKA
SÔ STYLE
Oki-Fune
also: ***Tomaribune,*** boat at anchor

Plants   sweet Williams
            Celastrus orbiculatus
Container Tsuri-fune, hanging bamboo ship

Plants   Japanese bell-flower *(Campanula japonica)*
Container Oki-fune, ship carved out of an old
            piece of wood

This ship arrangement, which is placed on a table, cupboard or in the tokonoma, is called Oki-fune or tomaribune and depicts a boat at anchor in a harbour. The sails have been hauled down. The basic mood of this ikebana style is one of peace.

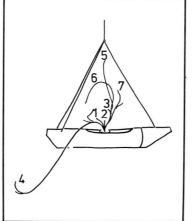

**The parts of
the arrangement**
1 Tai (sweet William)
2 Tai-Ashirai (sweet
    William)
3 Tai-Ashirai (sweet
    William)
4 Ro (rudder) (celastrus)
5 Shin (celastrus)
6 Shin-Ashirai
    (celastrus)
7 Soe (celastrus)

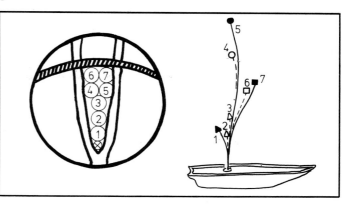

153

Plants   celastrus
            dahlias
Container   small basket mounted on a board

A lovely arrangement which creates a pleasant atmosphere everywhere. A container which has such an archaic effect can be acquired or made anywhere in Europe. Suibachi, an element of the composition serves to hold the basket in place and protects the wall from water spots.

    The branches here are arranged in such a way that they make the most agreeable effect when viewed from the front. Such hanging arrangements are called muko-gake in contrast to other compositions of the same kind which are better viewed from the side (yoko-gake).

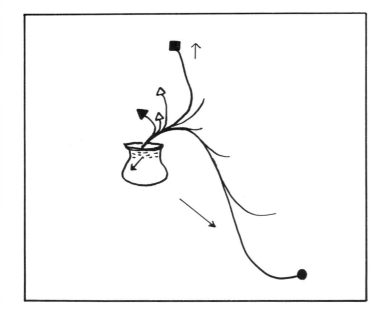

Plants   juniper branches
Container   simple bamboo container
             (Shishi-Guchi — lion mouth container)

You will notice that such a container can, with a little bit of skill, be made with a saw. It is enjoyable to be able to make new ikebana vases out of the versatile and appealing natural bamboo. Copying traditional styles can occasion individual creativity.

    This arrangement was created by the Master of the Saga School, Shishû Kobayashi of Kyôto.

155

MODERN AND CLASSICAL RIKKA

What is Rikka?

Rikka used to be called *Tatebana,* which means 'arranged, standing, upright flowers'. In our excursion into the history of ikebana at the beginning of this book, we saw that Rikka is the oldest form of Japanese flower arrangement, Rikka is both the foundation and root of ikebana. It is the most difficult and complicated art form in this area, it comprises seven or nine main elements and stands on a pillar shaped base.

Rikka has constantly changed in the course of its long history. In the twentieth century, new styles of Rikka have been created which are suitable for the times. In 1958, Ikenobô laid down the rules governing today's Rikka (Gendai-Rikka) and the small Rikka (Shohin-Rikka).

Containers used in modern Rikka

1 Ceramic vase
2 Ceramic cup with short base
3 Ceramic cup with long base
4 Ceramic cup with large water surface
5 Ceramic container with two feet
6 Ceramic bowl in form of a ship
7 Shallow ceramic bowl with feet
8 Shallow, square shaped water basin, suiban or sunabachi

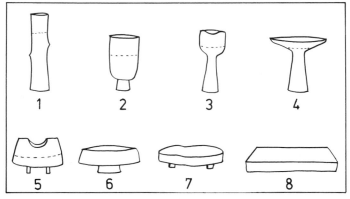

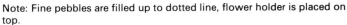

Note: Fine pebbles are filled up to dotted line, flower holder is placed on top.

Complete Rikka styles

A. Koten Rikka (classical Rikka)

1. Sugu-Shin-Style (Rikka with straight Shin)

2. Noki-Jin-Style (Rikka with curved, lively Shin)
   a) to e) see figure
   a) Jôdan-No-Rikka (Shin branches in an upper position -a- from central axis)
   b) Tsune-No-Rikka (Shin branches off at normal position -b- from central axis)
   c) Chûdan-No-Rikka (Shin branches off at middle position -c- from central axis)
   d) Gedan-No-Rikka (Shin branches off at lower position -d- from central axis)
   e) Mizugiwa-No-Rikka (Shin branches off at position next to water surface -e- from central axis)

3. Sunano-Mono-Style (Rikka in a basin filled with sand)
   a) Hitokabu-ike-Rikka (single group Rikka)
   b) Futakabu-ike-Rikka (double group Rikka)

4. Dôzuka-style (low, wide style of Rikka with two parallel Shin elements facing each other)

B. Gendai-Rikka (today's Rikka, modern Rikka)

1. Sugu-Shin-Style (Rikka with lively straight Shin)

2. Noki-Jin-Style (Rikka with lively Shin)
   a) Jôdan-No-Rikka (Shin branches off at upper position from central axis, see sketch)
   b) Chûdan-No-Rikka (Shin branches off in the middle -c- from central axis, see sketch)
   c) Gedan-No-Rikka (Shin branches off below -d- from the central axis)

3. Sunano-Mono-Style (Rikka in a sand basin)
   a) Hitokabu-ike-Rikka (one group Rikka)
   b) Futakabu-ike-Rikka (two group Rikka)

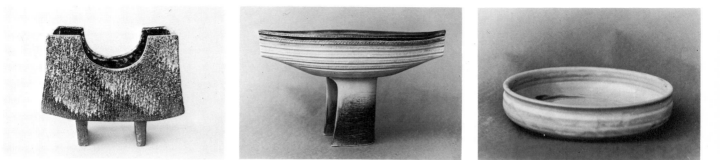

Containers for modern Rikka

1, 2   Bowl with feet
5, 6, 7 Ceramic cup
3, 4   Ceramic bowl

Containers for Modern Rikka

| 8 | 9 | 10 |

8 Glass vase
9 Tsubo (ceramic)
10 Ceramic cup

| 6 |
| 7 |

Containers for classical Rikka

1 Ganryûmimi, bronze
2 Marukanmimi, bronze
3 Sonshiki, bronze
4 Futakugata, bronze
5 Sunabachi, bronze
6 Sunabachi, bronze
7 Sunabachi, bronze

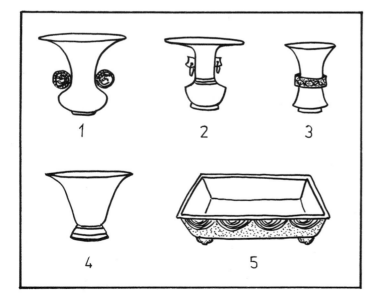

The nine main elements of a Rikka arrangement

The individual elements (yakueda) here as well as in the lessons have been numbered 1–9 which makes them easy to find in the diagrams and composition sketches.

1 Shin (truth, heart; earlier — God and faith)
2 Shôshin (Shô — correct; true Shin)
3 Dô (trunk, body)
4 Mae-Oki (Mae — front; Oku — to lay, place; front piece)
5 Soe (support, aid)
6 Hikae (reserve, abstinence)
7 Mikoshi (Miru — to see; Kosu — to move over something; long view)
8 Uke (receiving part; Uke appeals to movement and expression of the Shin part)
9 Nagashi (Nagasu — to pour out; Nagareru — flowing, flowing away, streaming; flowing lines, stream)

Directions of the nine main elements (see figures)

1 Shin usually stretches upwards.
2 Shôshin also stands upright and reaches almost to the middle of the composition.
3 Dô (seen from the side in sketch at bottom) turns towards the front.
4 Mae-Oki (also shown separately at bottom) comes towards the front.
5 Soe slants to the back left.
6 Hikae turns towards the left side.

7 Mikoshi slants to the back right.
8 Uke moves towards the right side.
9 Nagashi slants to the right front.

At the end of each of the elements, a symbol indicates direction by means of an arrow. Just as with the other ikebana styles, Rikka can also be arranged in a mirror image of this model. In addition, there are, as one can imagine, numerous variations of this basic style. One of the charms of Rikka is the unlimited number of possible variations and this is the reason why this style has been cultivated down through the centuries to today. Rikka continually offers new occasions for creativity and, in spite of the difficulties involved, is still the aim of many ikebana enthusiasts today.

The base positions in Rikka

The sketch shows the position of the individual main elements in a holder. Plant stems without markings are fillers for the main elements, while those stems marked with crosses serve to beautify the base, as this should always appear round. The stem marked with a U is a plant used to improve the back of the arrangement (ushiro-gakoi).

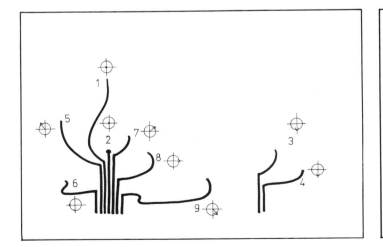

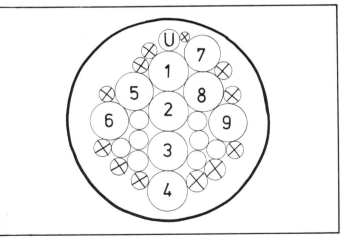

159

Twelve practical tips for arrranging Modern Rikka

1. When choosing floral materials for shin, you must proceed with caution, as the rest of the composition takes its cue from the style, line, character, attitude, colour, etc. of this element.

2. Nagashi has to have a really flowing line. For this reason you must choose a plant which has this quality.

3. Plants used for shôshin must have a strong enough character to be able to represent the middle of the composition. The plants must be able to express clearly the facts that shôshin is the heart of Rikka. For this role, the following noble plants are most suitable: irises, roses, peonies, lilies, calla.

4. Mikoshi and uke are always placed between shin and nagashi. For this reason they are, in their expression and form, dependent upon these elements. In some cases, mikoshi or uke or both can be omitted.

5. Soe and hikae are placed on the side opposite nagashi and uke, after the outward curving shin. Both of these elements should support shin while remaining themselves reserved. If shin is very strong or expressive, soe or hikae or both can be omitted.

6. Dô is the body of Rikka and consequently arranged not as a line but in mass. Today dô is no longer arranged in such a massive, thick way as previously.

7. Mae-oke lies closest to the observer and should, therefore, have a beautiful, clear form. It can be formed out of a mass of plants which harmonizes in colour with the rest of the composition. Often leaves or blossoms having a clear form serve as mae-oki.

8. The Rikka base is very important. All lines and stems of the composition should first stretch upwards together as if part of a single trunk, only then should they separate. The individual expression of each Rikka element develops out of the common upward striving whole. These elements must, however, adapt themselves harmoniously to the entire composition unless one wants purposely to portray disharmony.

9. The lines of Rikka should bend away sharply from the 'trunk'. Rikka arrangements in general appear to be somewhat more angular, edged and masculine than, for example, Shôka which has softer more curved lines.

10. Please be careful not to make your Rikka flat. The lines and parts stretch out in all directions giving a plastic, spatial effect.

11. Very important, of course, is a harmonious combination of floral arrangement and container.

12. All devices used in the composition such as wire, floral tape or bast, etc., should be hidden from view.

Heavy metal ring used to steady the base of Rikka

Kenzan in a heavy metal ring

Metal ring to support base placed on a kenzan

Tools and equipment for Rikka

1 Saw
2 Axe
3 Knife
4 Pointed gimlet
5 Hammer
6 Chisel
7 Screwdriver
8 Pliers
9 Various nails, pins and pegs
10 Electric drill
11 Various kinds of wire
12 Komiwara, straw bundle which can serve as flower holder especially for classical Rikka. First put together a small bunch tying these together to form a bundle which fits into the Rikka vase. The individual stems are then inserted into this.

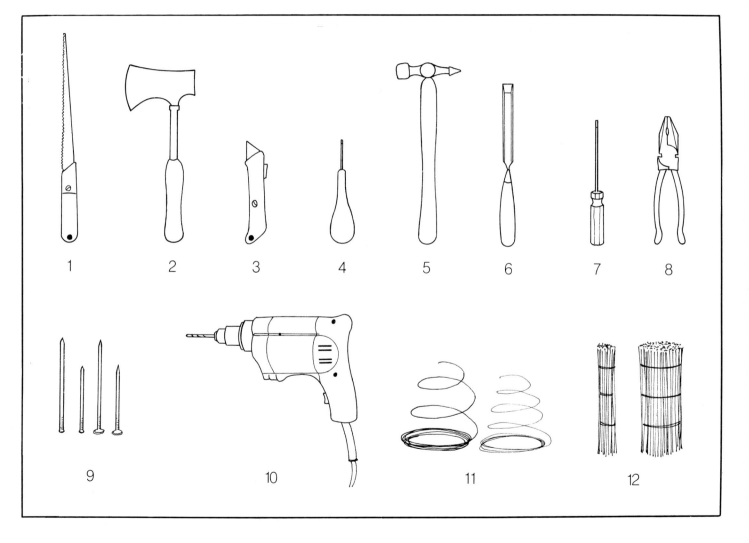

1   2   3   4   5   6   7   8

9   10   11   12

Plants	millet	Shin (1), Soe (5), Mikoshi (7)
	small sunflowers	Shin-filler
	lily	Shôshin (2)
	chrysanthemums	Dô (3)
	weigelie	Nagashi (9)
	juniper	Mae-Oki (4)
	withered Michaelmas daisy	Hikae (6)
Container	blue-green ceramic cup with feet	

Here autumn is portrayed. In place of the millet, pampas grass, or miscanthus sinensis can be used.

Create another Sugu-Shin arrangement using gladiolas as shin.

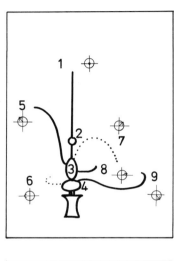

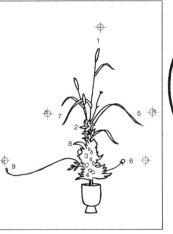

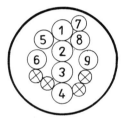

Diagram of the
Sugu-Shin Style

1	Shin	6	Hikae
2	Shôshin	7	Mikoshi
3	Dô	8	Uke
4	Mae-Oki	9	Nagashi
5	Soe		

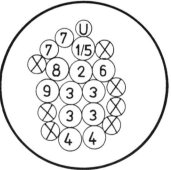

Diagram of
base position

Composition sketch
and base position
of this modern Rikka

Plants	hazel branches	Shin (1)
	pine	Soe (5), Hikae (6)
	white and red carnations	Shôshin (2), Dô (3)
	pampas grass, dried	Dô (3)
	red dogwood branches	Nagashi (9)
	dried fruit skins	Mae-Oki (4)
	bleached belvedere	Uke (8)
Container	black ceramic cup	

Winter Rikka. Here dry material is used because at this time of year in Europe there are few green branches and fewer flowers. When using dried flowers be sure to use a variety whereby a harmonious graduation of colour is realized.

163

Plants

day-lily leaves	Shin (1), Soe (5)	
corkscrew willow	Nagashi (9)	
white bell-flower	Shôshin (2)	
Japanese iris	Dô (3)	
maple branches	Dô (3)	
gerbera	Dô (3)	
calla leaves	Uke (8)	
funkia leaves	Mae-Oki (4)	
bleached Japanese fern	Mikoshi (7)	

Container Japanese ceramic cup with brown-white design

Arrange the composition on a large round kenzan.

The lily leaves for this lively shin (1) are placed behind the middle of the holder.

Then follow the willow branches of nagashi (2) which slant towards the front right.

We place two bell-flowers as shôshin (3) in the middle in front of shin.

Here irises, gerbera, and maple leaves serve as dô (4, 5) which then turn up again in hikae (6).

On the right side behind nagashi (2) a calla leaf (7) serves as uke.

Delicate ferns serve as mikoshi (9) filling the space at the back and two large funkia leaves (8) form the closing element in the front (mae-oki).

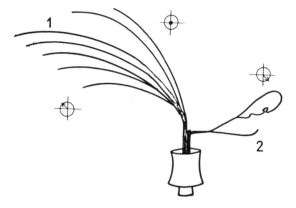

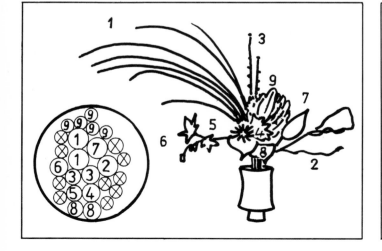

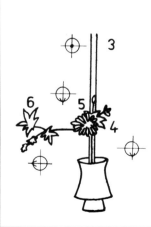

164

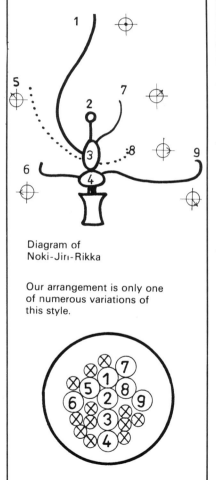

Diagram of
Noki-Jin-Rikka

Our arrangement is only one
of numerous variations of
this style.

165

Plants	spindle-tree	Shin (1), Nagashi (9)
	pampas grass	Dô (3)
	gladiolas	Soe (5)
	blue irises	Shôshin (2), Uke (8)
	red roses	Dô (3), Mae-Oki (4)
	pine	Dô (3)
	funkia leaves	Ushiro-Gakoi (1)
Container	blue ceramic cup	

Spindle-tree branches are easily bent. With these branches we create a Rikka with a lively shin (noki-jin) (1), turning jauntily to the left.

For nagashi (9) we use the same sturdy branches and bend them to the front right.

As shô-shin (2) we employ an iris giving it a background made of pampas grass (7).

Underneath the shin branches several gladiola buds gleam supported by a finely curved leaf (5). This soe-group turns to the back left.

Right, between shôshin and nagashi, an iris bud with leaves appears as uke (8).

The three roses composing dô are cut to various lengths and bend to the front (3).

The three gladiola leaves leaning out to the left form hikae (6). They have various lengths, but are shorter than the soe leaf.

Between the roses and to the front, we place as closing element (mae-oki) dark green pine branches (4). As ushiro-gakoi we place a funkia leaf behind shin (1).

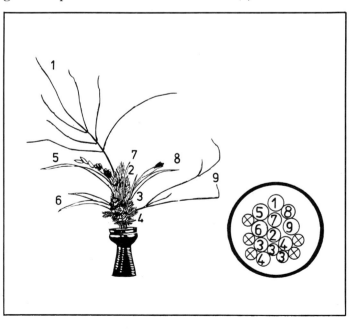

166

Plants	autumn red spiraea	Shin (1), Nagashi (9), Uke (8)
	liatris	Mikoshi (7)
	pampas grass	Dô (3)
	carnations	Shô-Shin (2)
	montbretia leaves	Soe (5)
	chrysanthemums	Dô (3), Mae-Oki (4)
		Hikae (6)
	juniper	Dô (3)
Container	Ceramic cup with light glaze	

The beautifully coloured leaves and fine lines of the spiraea are well suited for an autumn Rikka. We use these branches for shin (1), nagashi (9) and uke (8).

The gentle montbretia leaves harmonize well with the above (5). Pampas grass is good as background material (3)

bringing out the best in the gleaming red carnations (2) and chrysanthemums (3, 4).

This kind of Rikka is somewhat difficult to arrange. But one should often practise the Noki-Jin style with some clear branches as this influences one's ability to create Moribana, Nageire and Shôka.

Plants   Turk's cap
lily leaves
German irises
plum branches
gerbera
peony leaves
Container   ship-style bowl with feet, ceramic

In this summer arrangement, shin and uke are made of the same material. We have used a special flower here, the pyramid lily.

Possible variations can be made with other flowers such as larkspur, monk's-hood, fleur-de-lis, foxglove, liatris, eremurus, gladiola — blooming twig or berry branch.

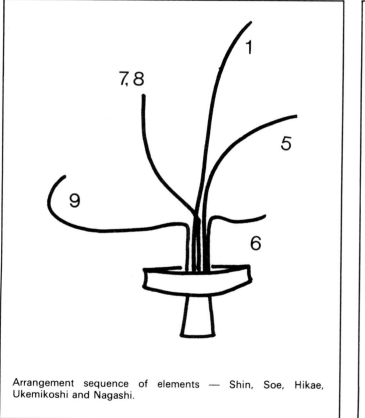

Arrangement sequence of elements — Shin, Soe, Hikae, Ukemikoshi and Nagashi.

The Shôshin, Dô, Mae-Oki group seen from the front and from the side, Dô and Mae-Oki turn to the front.

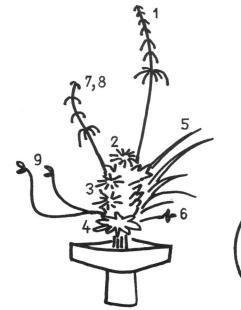

Sketch of composition

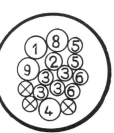

Base position

1 Shin   1 Turk's cap
2 Shôshin   1 gerbera
3 Dô   2 gerbera and 3 peony leaves
4 Mae-Oki   1 peony leaf
5 Soe   lily leaves
6 Hikae   1 yellow iris with leaves
7, 8 Ukemikoshi   1 pyramid lily
9 Nagashi   1 plum branch

169

Plants	willow branches	Shin (1), Soe (5)
	dark blue irises	Shôshin (2)
	peonies	Dô (3)
	five funkia leaves	Mae-Oki (4), Uke (8)
	five grasses	Mikoshi (7)
	five gladiola leaves	Nagashi (9)
	large leaf cotoneaster	Hikae (6)
Container	large, brown ceramic bowl with feet	

We bend the wild willow branches into a large elegant bow (1). We pull off most of the leaves because they wither very quickly.

The leaves placed to the left as nagashi are bent and held in place with flower wire (9).

The irises (2) serving as shôshin and the peonies with two leaves serving as dô (3) are placed in the middle.

The large, fleshy funkia leaves again make up the front of the composition.

The grass (7) slants to the back as do the two funkia leaves (8).

One small cotoneaster branch is enough to balance the right hand side.

To the rear, not visible in the picture, we employ a further funkia leaf as ushiro-gakoi.

Soe is not represented by an individual branch, as it is included in shin.

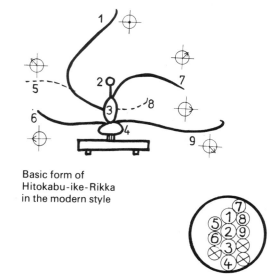

Basic form of
Hitokabu-ike-Rikka
in the modern style

Base position

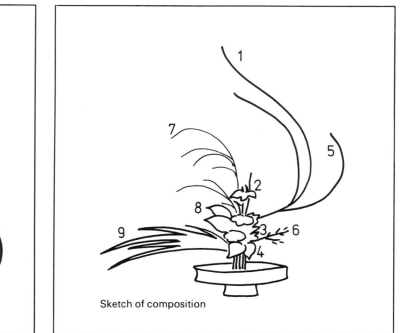

Sketch of composition

Base position of
the Rikka shown here

171

Plants	corn *(Zea mays)*	Shin (1), Mikoshi (7)
	roses	Shôshin (2)
	cotoneaster	Hikae (6)
	chrysanthemums	Dô (3)
	forsythia	Uke (8), Nagashi (9)
	pine	Dô (3)
	funkia leaves	Ushiro-Gakoi
Container	large, deep blue ceramic basin	

Corn has large, impressive leaves and if you cut it before it is ripe, it has an umbrella shaped blossom on top. Corn grows everywhere but has rarely been used as an ikebana material.

Dahlias or asters match the season.

After having completed the arrangement, we fill the basin with clean, suitably coloured, fine pebbles.

Diagram of basic form with base positions

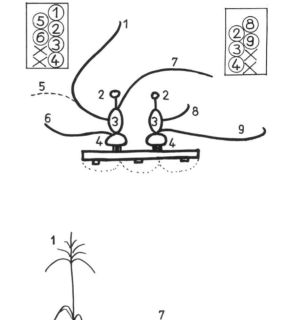

Plants	New Zealand flax	Shin (1)
	irises	Shôshin (2)
	orange gerbera with leaves	Dô (3), Soe (5), Mae-Oki (4)
	privet	Hikae (6)
	bleached wisteria reeds	Shin (1), Nagashi (9)
	calla with leaves	Shôshin (2), Dô (3), Mae-Oki (4)
	daisies	Dô (3), Mae-Oki (4)
Container	ceramic cup with design	

This style having two shin elements must be arranged carefully and in a slender manner. Mikoshi (7) and uke (8) are represented by a single calla leaf.

Variations with other plants

As shin, you can try gladiolas, mullein, allium, or liatris. The two plants chosen should not have the same character.

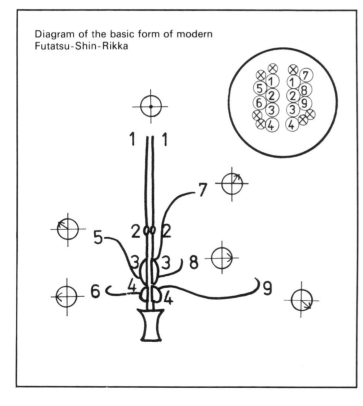

Diagram of the basic form of modern Futatsu-Shin-Rikka

173

Plants   pheasant feathers
bird-of-paradise flower with leaves
feather cypress
decorative asparagus
fan-palm leaf, dried
Container slender ceramic cup

This arrangement was created by Professor Kôshû Murata for the Ikebana exhibition at the National Museum in Tokyo.

FREE STYLE

The free style allows one to create an individualized composition which says more about the personal characteristics of the person creating the arrangement. For this reason, the following arrangements should serve more as an inspiration to your own creative abilities than as models to be copied directly.

Fern and yellow carnations in a light brown ceramic cup.

'By the Sea'
A shallow table arrangement composed of a water-lily blossom, the leaves from water-lilies and irises and one small spiraea branch.

A gentle spring arrangement for the Ikebana exhibition in the National Museum in Tokyo made of bleached mitsumata branches, daffodils, a special kind of decorative asparagus and leaves of Eriobotrya japonica.

An arrangement rich in contrasts and having an interesting linear movement by Shusui Kato (Ikenobô) for the Ikebana exhibition in the National Museum, Tokyo. This arrangement is composed of white feathers, plastic strips, lily leaves and three reed mace (bulrush).

'Forbidden View'
New Zealand flax, sunflowers, reeds (Smilax chinensis), mountain ash leaves.

 85   87

86   88

'Together'
Black cup with open tulips, carnations, and the leaves of Fatsia japonica.

'Power'
Cherry tree trunk with a blossoming shoot, gladiolas and anthurium arranged between large pebbles for the Ikebana exhibition in the Staatliches Museum für Völkerkunde in Munich, by Horst Pointner.

'Waves'
Dried lotus capsules, plastic strips, poppies, vetches (exhibition in National Museum Tokyo).

89 90
91

'Flying'
Plastic straws, feathers, orchid blossoms (cattleya), dwarf pine branch, spiral shaped wire (exhibition in National Museum Tokyo).

'Melody'
This free style arrangement was composed by Anneliese Vitense for the Ikenobô exhibition in the Staatliches Museum für Völkerkunde, Munich. She used only three gerbera and larch branches.

92

華への展開
いけばな池坊展   村田弘洲

This last arrangement was created by my most honoured teacher, Professor Kôshû Murata for the National Museum Tokyo.

It demonstrates what great feeling for plants is necessary even in a very free style Ikebana. Here the gentle violet hidden under the front roots is repeated in the background by means of two lights hidden at the back of the composition.

The Japanese are very open to creative attempts influenced by Western aesthetic principles, and here in the West, people are turning increasingly to the positive achievements of Eastern culture. This is what we hope to achieve by this book: A conciliation of Eastern and Western culture, a joining of tradition and progress, simplicity but strength, naturalness and harmony, a harmonious relationship between man and nature and between man and his environment, harmony of thought and desire, and peace through 'flower hearts'.

We mean this without pathos. We don't mean it in an abstract manner, and we wish it for our children.

PRACTICAL TIPS FOR IKEBANA

How to keep flowers and branches fresh

Being able to keep flowers and branches fresher longer and mastering all possible technical tricks does not mean that one is able to create ikebana. These methods are also used by florists. Ikebana is more than a practical, decorative arrangement of flowers. Keeping flowers fresher longer is not the main objective of ikebana, as it is in commercial floral arrangements which are sold in stores. One of the central aspects of ikebana is the emphasizing of the short duration and the natural process of maturing and passing away of plant life.

For almost a thousand years, great ikebana masters have given their protégés secret recipes on how to keep plants alive longer. Such tips are very important for ikebana exhibitions, although each individual master has to gain knowledge through his own personal experience since each plant has its own characteristics which change in response to location and type of soil. Flowers grown in greenhouses have to be handled differently from those raised in gardens. Tropical flowers cannot be prepared like mountain plants. Even the same kind of plants absorb water and nutrients differently.

For this reason, the following tips gathered in working with plants should only serve as a general guideline. Everyone has to find out for himself through practical experience which methods are best for certain flowers. Flowers are living things just like ourselves. When they are treated with care they thank us by remaining fresher longer.

In this survey the most important physical and chemical methods of keeping flowers fresh have been assembled. Sometimes the life of cut flowers can be doubled.

TIP	valid for:
1. When possible, cut plants early in the morning, in the evening or on rainy-days. Avoid cutting in the midday sun.	all plants
2. Avoid cutting plants on dry, windy days.	all plants
3. If you want to do something good for the plants, then pour water over them while cutting.	all plants
4. Whenever possible, carry the plants home in a damp cloth. This prevents premature drying out.	all plants; be careful with delicate blossoms and stamens.
5. Always use very sharp garden shears or Ikebana shears with two cutting blades. The so-called rose shears are unsuitable for detailed work and delicate plants. They crush the vessels.	all flowers, grasses and leaves
6. Store flowers in a cool, dark room or in opaque foil until you are ready to begin your arrangement.	all plants
7. Place flowers and branches in deep water for a few hours before working with them.	all flowers

179

TIP	valid for:	TIP	valid for:
8. Remove as soon as possible all dead leaves and secondary sprouts which are not needed for the composition. They evaporate too much water.	most leafy branches and flowers; especially branches with young leaves	15. Cut the plants thoroughly once or twice underwater before arranging them. In this way air bubbles cannot force their way into the vessels.	all plants but especially: mimosa, asters, cornflowers, fleur-de-lis, dahlias, marsh marigold, bell-flower, caladium, centaurea, etc.
9. Cut off a 1–2 cm rim from very large leaves with sharp Ikebana shears. This increases the capillary effect.	for example the leaves of philodendron, etc.		
10. Whenever possible use boiled or stale water. It contains less bacteria and less dissolved air that would form bubbles and block the vessels.	most plants	16. The hollow stems of some plants can be filled with water by means of a special pump or a bicycle pump.	lotus, water-lilies, bamboo, marsh marigold
11. Clean all Ikebana containers carefully removing mud and algae deposits. In this way you protect your materials from decay.		17. Spray the arrangement several times a day with distilled water. This is especially important in heated rooms.	most plants but not orchids
12. Clean your kenzan regularly before beginning work. You can use a needle, an old brush, or a kenzan-naoshi — a tool for straightening out the needles of the flower holder.		18. Make sure that the room is properly humidified. An electric humidifier is very handy.	all plants
13. Shears, saws and knives should be clean.		19. Some plants cannot stand contact with iron. For this reason they are not cut but rather broken.	chrysanthemums
14. Make sure that as little decayed material as possible is in the water.	leafy branches flower petals	20. If purchased flowers are already a bit flabby, you can improve them by placing them up to their heads in boiled water for 2 to 3 hours. First cut them under water.	most flowers and branches especially roses

TIP	valid for:	TIP	valid for:
21. Place flowers in lukewarm water and let them rest, only then arrange.	faded flowers	28. If you put ice-cubes in the water — but not in the water of the freshening up bath — the flowers will not fade so quickly, and decay-inducing bacteria will not form so quickly.	summer flowers like dahlias, or zinnias
22. Should you want to freshen flowers by showering them, do so with the flower head away from the water, so that the stem and flower are moistened but the flower is not destroyed.	cut flowers and leafy branches	29. Some plants freshen up quicker when the bark is pealed off at the cut end by about 2–3 cm.	leafy branches, chrysanthemums
23. Some flowers have to be cut on a slant before the 'refreshing' bath. This is best done with a very sharp knife or good ikebana shears.	roses, flowers after long transport without water	30. There are branches which should be sharpened like a pencil before arranging them.	branches, twigs
24. The absorption surface can be increased by cutting slits 2–4 cm long at the cut end.	branches, flowers for arrangement	31. The cut edge of several plants can be held for 1–2 minutes in almost boiling water. Woody stems can stand 5 minutes of this treatment, but softer stems can only tolerate water at 50° C. The rest of the plant must be protected from the heat and from the hot steam by means of a damp cloth.	thistles, dahlias, peonies, Salomon's seal, 'milk' secreting plants like the spurge, be careful with: chrysanthemums, clivia, daffodils, roses
25. For some branches it is a good idea to tap the cut surface. To do this, one should use the handle or back of the Ikebana shears.	woody branches, chrysanthemums		
26. Remove decaying pieces immediately and change water. Decay-inducing bacteria increase very quickly. Decaying plants secrete ethyl gas which causes further decay.	all plants	32. Stems secreting milk can be singed at the cut edge. Be careful to protect the rest of the plant from the candle gas flame or lighter by using a damp piece of cloth or paper. After this, place the stem immediately in water so that the singed cut edge can absorb water.	spurge, rubber tree
27. Change the water every day. It is easy when you use a hand pump or a simple, thin, rubber tube.	all ikebana		

TIP	valid for:	TIP	valid for:
33. Spraying with hair spray or florist spray prevents too rapid drying out.	bamboo, large-leaved tropical plants	38. The dampened cut edge of some flowers can be placed in alum powder (double salt, sulphate of potassium and sulphate of aluminium).	*Wisteria sinensis,* dahlias, peonies
34. Florists offer a variety of products to keep flowers fresh. You have to try them yourself to find out which solutions are best for which flowers since water composition and flower quality are always different. The solution is added to the water according to the directions of the manufacturer. In this way decay-inducing bacteria are prevented and a bit of fertilizer is added.	certain plants; follow manufacturers' instructions	39. A few minutes in vinegar help another group of plants to stay fresher longer.	reeds, bamboo, miscanthus
		40. The ability of plants to absorb water can be increased by placing the stems in water in which ashes have been stirred.	campanella
		41. A very good stimulant is peppermint oil. The cut edge is submerged in it for a short time.	daisies
35. Stems which have been tapped can be rubbed with cooking salt on the cut edge. Place plants immediately in freshening up bath for several hours.	roses, bell-flowers	42. Other plants react better to the spicy juice of peperoni.	grasses
36. A solution made of a half a cup of water and 2 teaspoons of table salt can be used as a stimulant. The stems are placed in this solution for 1–2 minutes, then in deep fresh water for 1–2 hours before being placed in an arrangement.	roses, bell-flowers	43. It is very difficult to keep bamboo fresh. You can try to boil the ends in a solution made of two heaped teaspoons of salt and one-quarter litre water. Take care to protect the rest of the plant. Rub the leaves on both sides with sugar water so that they don't roll up so quickly. Finally make a hole in the walls between the knots of the tubes and fill the segments with boiling salt solution.	bamboo
37. Some plants can be placed in a 'freshening up' bath of alcohol (medical alcohol, gin). The cut edge is dried with a cloth beforehand.	maple branches, poppies, mimosa, thistles, caladium, gerbera		

How to bring about early sprouting

The following branches sprout even in winter when placed in water for 1–2 weeks in a heated but not too dry room: forsythia, Japanese quince, cherry, apple and plum trees, and because of their delicate leaves: lime, birch, spiraea, beech, chestnut or whitethorn branches. It is best to place the branches in lukewarm water for several hours beforehand and then to sprinkle them with water from time to time.

How to dry flowers

When we speak of ikebana, we mean principally the art of arranging living flowers and we would like to avoid using 'mummified' flowers as much as possible except as a contrast to living plants. Nevertheless here are a few tips. The blossoms of most flowers keep their colour when dried if the following steps are observed. The stems are cut off and then placed in a hermetically sealed container. This is filled with drying powder (silica gel) and kept closed for one to two weeks. It is essential that the drying powder covers the entire flower and penetrates the spaces between the petals. Wire and florist's tape then serve as stems.

How to preserve autumn branches

Collect the branches in early autumn, tap the fibrous cut-end, or cut into it several times and place it in a mixture of two-thirds water and one-third glycerol. In the course of three weeks the leaves lose their colour and can then be stored for months in a dry, dust-free place.

The 20 largest ikebana schools

There are approximately 3000 ikebana schools. The largest of them teach more than a million students a year. Several have won recognition all over Japan and in many foreign countries as well. They maintain their own academies. The school's style is strongly influenced by its traditions and the work of its leading ikebana masters. The present director of the Ikenobô School, Ikenobô Senei, is the successor of Onono Imoko who in the seventh century brought the tradition of flower sacrifices for Buddha from China to Japan. The history of ikebana is in many respects the history of Ikenobô. But modern ikebana and experimental compositions are also developed by the Headmaster and his team of able artists. Ohara Hôun today directs the school founded by his grandfather in 1911, and Teshigahara Sôfû, another famous ikebana master of our times, founded his own Sôgetsu-School in 1926.

For those interested in learning about ikebana, this list represents the 20 artistically most important schools.

1. Ikenobô
2. Sôgetsu-Ryû
3. Ohara-Ryû
4. Adachi-Ryû
5. Ikenobô-Ryûsei-Ha
6. Saga-Go-Ryû
7. Shôgetsudô-Koryû
8. Kiryû-Shôtô-Kai
9. Koryû-Shôô-Kai
10. Mishô-Ryû
11. Mishô-Ryû Bumpo-Kai
12. Ichyô-Shiki
13. Yamato-Kadô
14. Ikaruga-Ryû
15. Enshû-Ryû
16. Mimuro-Ryû
17. Shûhô-Ryû
18. Shin-Ikenobô
19. Sômi-Ryû
20. Shikusei-Ryû

IKEBANA LITERATURE

Averill, Mary: Japanese Flower Arrangement. London (John Lane The Bodley Head) w.y.

Carr, E. Rachel: Stepping Stones to Japanese Floral Art. Tokyo (News Service Ltd.) 1968

Davidson Georgie: Ikebana Simplified. London 1968

Fujiwara, Yûchiku: Rikka. Ikenobô Ikebana. Tokyo 1967

Fujiwara, Yûchiku: Ikenobô. Shôka Style. Tokyo 1970

Gordon-Allen, Ellen: Japanese Flower Arrangement in a Nutshell. Tokyo 1968

Ikenobô, Senei: Ikenobô-School. Best of Ikebana III. Tokyo 1974

Ikenobô, Senei: Ikebana. Osaka 1975

Ikenobô, Senei: Ikenobô, Nageïre, Moribana. Kyoto 1971

Ikenobô, Senei: Ikebana of Senei Ikenobô — Shôka Style. Tokyo 1974

Ishiyama, Fumie: Ikenobô. Ikebana for Living. Tokyo 1965

Koehn, Alfred: Japanese Classical Flower Arrangements. Tokyo — Rutland 1951

March-Penney, John: Japanese Flower Arrangement — Ikebana. London — New York — Sidney — Toronto 1969

Neese, Martha & Marvin: Fun with Flowers. Japanese Flower Arrangement Made Easy. Tokyo 1969

Nishikawa, Issotei: Floral Art of Japan. Tokyo 1959

Ohara, Hôun: Ohara School. Best of Ikebana II. Tokyo 1962

Ohno, Noriko: Typical Japanese Ikebana. Tokyo 1961

Richie, Donald/Weatherby, Meredith: The Master's Book of Ikebana. Tokyo 1966

Saga Gosho Sôshisho Gijutsuin: Saga School. Heika Style. Tokyo 1970

Sparnon, Norman: The Poetry of Leaves. Creative Ideas for Japanese Flower Arrangement. New York — Tokyo 1970

Sparnon, Norman: A Guide to Japanese Flower Arrangement. Tokyo w.y.

Teshigahara, Sôfû: The Art of Sofu. Ikebana, Calligraphy and Sculpture. Tokyo 1971

Wood, Mary Cokeley: Flower Arrangement — Art of Japan. Tokyo 1970